Psalm 32

Psalm 32

A Meditation

B. J. CONDREY

Foreword by Richard Brash

RESOURCE *Publications* · Eugene, Oregon

PSALM 32
A Meditation

Copyright © 2025 B. J. Condrey. All rights reserved. Except for brief quotations in critical publications or reviews, no part of this book may be reproduced in any manner without prior written permission from the publisher. Write: Permissions, Wipf and Stock Publishers, 199 W. 8th Ave., Suite 3, Eugene, OR 97401.

Resource Publications
An Imprint of Wipf and Stock Publishers
199 W. 8th Ave., Suite 3
Eugene, OR 97401

www.wipfandstock.com

PAPERBACK ISBN: 979-8-3852-5865-9
HARDCOVER ISBN: 979-8-3852-5866-6
EBOOK ISBN: 979-8-3852-5867-3
VERSION NUMBER 09/17/25

All Scripture quotations, unless otherwise indicated, are taken from the Holy Bible, New International Version®, NIV®. Copyright ©1973, 1978, 1984, 2011 by Biblica, Inc.™ Used by permission of Zondervan. All rights reserved worldwide. www.zondervan.comThe "NIV" and "New International Version" are trademarks registered in the United States Patent and Trademark Office by Biblica, Inc.™

Contents

Foreword by Richard Brash | vii
Preface | xi
Acknowledgments | xvii
Introduction | xix

Blessed | 1
Heavy | 17
Break | 27
Prayer | 39
Hiding Place | 45
Guidance | 55
Love | 65
Rejoice | 75

Bibliography | 81

Foreword

IT HAS BEEN SAID that reading Scripture is like collecting pollen, and meditating on it is like making honey.¹ My friend B.J. Condrey is both a reader and a meditator, a collector and a maker, and this book is another sweet fruit of his labors in the Word of God. But B.J. would be the first to admit that the sweetness to savor from Psalm 32 is foremost a gift: it is *God's* words that are truly "sweeter than honey".²

B.J. and I met when he came to my hometown of Edinburgh, Scotland, to begin Ph.D. research in Christian ethics, at the same time as I began doctoral work on the doctrine of Scripture. Our friendship grew over adjacent desks in the graduate study area, a shared concern for evangelical witness in the academy, and the desire to help one another to live for the glory of God wherever he might lead. Pursuing God's call to different parts of the world means we have not met in person for several years. But our online fellowship in prayer and mutual encouragement is an ongoing channel of God's grace to me. In addition, B.J.'s writings—whether autobiographical, philosophical, or devotional—are a gift for which I and many others are thankful.

---

1. This idea is attributed to Old Testament scholar Bruce Waltke in Kelly M. Kapic, *A Little Book for New Theologians: Why and How to Study Theology* (Downers Grove: IVP, 2012), 118.

2. Ps 119:103.

Foreword

What B.J. advocates in the introduction to this book—the first of a planned series of thoughtful and devotional meditations on the Psalms—is his personal approach to the daily reading of Scripture: slow, intentional, and expectant. In many respects, this is not a new idea. Some readers will appreciate its similarity to the ancient Christian practice of *lectio divina*: Christ-centered reading, meditating, prayer, and contemplation. Old is gold. This devotional Bible reading is exemplified in the eight meditations that follow. But in this book B.J. shows us that devotion need not be the enemy of serious intellectual engagement. Readers will find here rigorous theological thinking, deep reflection on the task of interpretation, and careful attention to matters of grammar and history. B.J. is in conversation with a range of interlocutors, from the Church Fathers through to the present day, on whose rich wisdom he draws.

Above all, however, B.J. reveals through these meditations that he is in conversation with God himself. Like Augustine, who loved Psalm 32, B.J. knows that Jesus speaks through the Psalter, and indeed that all of Holy Scripture is like a temple from which the Lord himself speaks by the Spirit.[3] B.J. has taken time to listen and to learn from the Lord. And he models what he teaches others. Like David before him, he is a practicing preacher, who *knows* that what he imparts is true not only because he *reads* it but because he has *experienced* it. Must believers be honest before God to enjoy true intimacy with him? Then hear the refreshing honesty of B.J.'s startling confession: "I spent 19 years of my Christian life miserable." And what of the remedy for such misery? Would you know the gift of all gifts: a clean conscience before a holy God? Then follow B.J. as he follows King David, through guilt, brokenness, God's fatherly chastisement, and the troubles that must come—even to believers—to

---

3. Augustine, *De Doctrina*, preface.

forgiveness, joy, and the certainty of acceptance in God's beloved Son. Hidden in him, we will never be utterly overcome.

The choice of Psalm 32 to begin this series of books is an "inspired" one (if I may use that term in the general sense) because, as B.J. recognizes, this Psalm of David "bears the watermark of the cross" perhaps like no other. It is, as he acknowledges, "a microcosm of the gospel", showing us the way of blessing through the forgiveness that we are offered by Jesus Christ. Psalm 32 relates what the God of mercy does for repentant believers in his Son. But it also points us to what *we* must do in response. B.J.—ever the Christian ethicist and (increasingly?) the Augustinian—will not allow a reading of Scripture that does not lead us to love. The Word of God shapes us and calls for a life-changing response. This is how we enter—and press on—into the blessedness that God has prepared for those who love him.

Not all readers will agree with every voice or view in this book. Questions may remain. Not everyone will set their alarm for 5:30 AM tomorrow to follow a particular method: we are not all B.J.! But surely all Christian readers will be provoked and prompted to keep listening to the living God who continues to speak the words of the Bible to us, and to respond to him in pursuit of fullness of joy in our relationship with him. It is remarkable that in the Psalter we learn not only of the blessedness of believers, but also that believers are called to "bless" God in response (see 16:7, 26:12, 34:1, 103:1–2, 22, 104:1, 35, 115:18, 134:1–2, 135:19–21). As unworthy servants—and mere creatures at that—we cannot give God anything he does not already have or that he needs. And yet, made in his image and re-made in the image of his Son, we are to bless the God and Father of our Lord Jesus Christ who has blessed us beyond measure, today and always. Let this day be such a day!

Richard Brash

Preface

"This is how I read the Bible now. I ask of each passage: What is God saying to us here? And I ask God that he would help us hear what he wants to say."

~Dietrich Bonhoeffer

For the last few months, the local church we belong to has been without a pastor, and I have been asked to preach on occasion. It has been a privilege and an honor. Since completing my PhD in Scotland in May 2020, I've only preached once at a friend's church in Hattiesburg, Mississippi. But in the last three months, I've had the opportunity to preach four times.

This book grew out of one of my sermons in November 2024 when I spoke on "Living in the Psalms." For the past 10–15 years, The Book of Psalms have held a special place in my daily life through a spiritual discipline I developed. Most mornings, my routine begins like this:

1. Wake up around 5:30 AM
2. Walk to the kitchen
3. Grind the coffee beans for the day's chosen brew

4. Make two cups of coffee in my 17-ounce stainless steel French press
5. Settle into my home office, where a simple blue chair, a soft lamp, and a $10 solid wood side table (courtesy of Facebook Marketplace) await me
6. Read a psalm in a slow, prayerful, worshipful manner
7. Transition to the part of the Bible I'm focusing on in that season to read and meditate

I start with a psalm for a very intentional reason. In Matthew 6:9–13, Jesus teaches us to pray, beginning with, "Our Father in heaven, hallowed be your name. . ." Before asking for anything, we are to direct our attention and adoration to the Father in worship. This order is significant. Without it, our weak and fickle hearts tend to default to self-centeredness—focusing on our wants, perceived needs, and anxieties. Dietrich Bonhoeffer writes: "The first moments of the new day are not for the time for our own plans and worries, not even for our zeal to accomplish our own work, but for God's liberating grace, God's sanctifying presence."[1] Even prayer can become selfish when it begins with requests instead of worship.

To guard against this, I begin my time with the Lord by praying through a psalm. The Book of Psalms helps still my heart, orient my focus toward God rather than myself, and provides language for prayer. Dietrich Bonhoeffer writes, "The disciples want to pray, but they do not know how to do it. That can be very painful, to want to speak with God and not be able to. . ."[2] The Psalms are truly a gift—an antidote to what Bonhoeffer calls the "agony of prayerlessness." What sincere disciple has not, at some point, grieved over their

---

1. Bonhoeffer, *Meditating on the Word*, 38.
2. Bonhoeffer, *Psalms*, 14.

poverty in prayer? I know I have. And yet, deep in my heart, I long to be able to say with David: "but I am a man of prayer."[3]

But I do not turn to just any random psalm; I follow a simple method. For instance, if I read Psalm 1 today, I let it guide my worship and help direct my heart toward God. This might take five minutes or thirty, depending on how the Spirit leads. As I read, I pause at words, phrases, or verses that stand out, trusting that the Holy Spirit is ministering through them. I don't rush or read through the psalm first and return later to what stood out—I've learned that this approach doesn't work as well. Instead, I sit with the word, phrase, or verse, meditating until I sense the Spirit is finished. I then pick up and start reading again.

Once I've finished the psalm, I make a small tally mark beside the chapter number in my Bible to indicate where I left off. The next morning, I begin with the next psalm. Over time, my Bibles have become marked with these simple tallies, showing how the Psalms have rooted and sustained me in my walk with God. I can't live without them.

This practice ensures my prayer time isn't dominated by worry, anxiety, or self-focus. Instead, it points my heart toward God—his written Word, his will, and whatever he might want to say. Bonhoeffer again is helpful here: "This is how I read the Bible now. I ask of each passage: What is God saying to us here? And I ask God that he would help us hear what he wants to say."[4] May we apply this piece of wisdom as we read and reflect on the words in Psalm 32.

When I preached, I shared this method after giving a more general introduction to the Psalms, hoping it might inspire others to engage with them in a similarly personal and transformative way. After introducing The Book of Psalms in

---

3. Ps 109:4
4. Bonhoeffer, *Meditating on the Word*, 45.

my sermon, I focused on Psalm 32. Preparing and preaching reminded me of how special this psalm is. *It is a microcosm of the Gospel of Jesus Christ.* I will say more about this in the Introduction. Roy Gingrich writes: "[Psalm 32] teaches the gospel more clearly than does any other Old Testament Scripture except the 53rd chapter of Isaiah."[5] The psalm captures the themes of forgiveness, the hard-heartedness we often cling to, the need for confession and repentance, and the breakthrough and subsequent joy that comes when we yield to God. Viewing Psalm 32 from this perspective—as a snapshot of the Gospel—reminds me of C.S. Lewis's words about the Christian faith:

> Christianity tells people to repent and promises them forgiveness. It therefore has nothing (as far as I know) to say to people who do not know they have done anything to repent of and who do not feel that they need any forgiveness . . . When you know you are sick, you will listen to the doctor.[6]

While this psalm is best read as addressing a Christian who, in hardhearted refusal, resists repentance and reconciliation with God, it can also be seen as a beautiful picture of the Gospel—the *euangelion*—and the journey of one coming to faith in Christ. Bonhoeffer writes: "[Jesus] bears the whole distance from God . . . suffering is overcome by suffering. Communion with God is granted precisely in [Christ's] suffering."[7]

One wonderful and hospitable characteristic of Psalm 32 is that it is strikingly honest. David resisted God. He clung to his sin, perhaps even wishing God would leave him alone. But God won. In an age dominated by social media, where

---

5. Gingrich, *The Book of Psalms*, 47.
6. Lewis, *Mere Christianity*, 35.
7. Bonhoeffer, *Discipleship*, 90.

PREFACE

so many strive to curate polished profiles that showcase only their strengths, the vulnerability and transparency of someone like David is refreshing—like a glass of cool water on a hot summer day. Psalm 32 reminds us that it's okay not to have it all together. As Jesus beautifully said, "It is not the healthy who need a doctor, but the sick."[8]

You'll notice an abundance of quotes from Dietrich Bonhoeffer's *Meditating on the Word*. Recently, a kindhearted lady in our church gifted me a bag of old books. To my surprise and delight, I discovered an extremely old hardback copy of this book. Over the past few years, I've read more Bonhoeffer than ever before, and I find him both fascinating and challenging. Through my evangelical lens, I sometimes wrestle with his ideas—not in a negative way, but as an opportunity to grow. I want to remain open, to be stretched, and never to assume that I—or my particular theological perspective—have everything figured out. As soon as I got home, I pulled out this book and started reading. I haven't been able to put it down, which is why you'll see it quoted often.

After the sermon, another lady approached me and said, "I have never read the Psalms, and I am now going to start." Her words stirred a mix of emotions in me—heartbreak on one hand, but deep encouragement on the other. My hope in writing this book is to inspire you to make the Psalms a central part of your life moving forward.

Eat them.

Drink them.

Embrace them.

8. Matt. 9:12

Preface

I pray that the Lord will use this book not only to enrich your reading of Psalm 32, but also to awaken a deeper appreciation for all of the Psalms and lead you into a richer experience of them—one that transforms your life. The Psalms are like a table where a very real God meets the very real us—warts and all. As Wayne Grudem rightly notes: "The words of Scripture are the words by which we nourish our spiritual lives."[9] This is definitely true of the Psalms, an endless well of living water from which we can drink anytime. As you read this book, have your Bible open to Psalm 32. Go back and forth between this book and the words of Scripture. Read slowly. Pause frequently. Ask the generous and illuminating Holy Spirit to open your eyes. Ultimately, my prayer for you is that you meet Christ in this psalm and spend the rest of your life exploring the depths and mining the treasures that await throughout the Psalms. They are truly beautiful and possess the power to make our lives beautiful for our Lord's pleasure and glory.

---

9. Grudem, *Systematic Theology*, 54.

Acknowledgments

To my friend, Dr. Richard Brash—thank you for your willingness to read an early chapter and offer thoughtful, encouraging feedback. Your insights were both helpful and appreciated.

To my wife, Allison—thank you for always encouraging me to follow my heart in writing.

Introduction

"Augustine, who like his master Paul was keenly aware of his own desires both to be a saint and to be a sinner, cherished this psalm."[1]

~Michael Wilcock

I WAS TWENTY-SEVEN WHEN a book profoundly reshaped my life. *Grace Works* by Dudley Hall came to me at just the right time—one of those moments when you sense the hand of God guiding even the smallest details. I tell more of the story in another book, *Heal Me or Kill Me*, but what I can say here is that through Hall's words, the Lord broke the suffocating chains of obsessive-compulsive disorder (OCD) that had long held me captive. At the same time, he freed my heart from the exhausting burden of trying to earn his love and approval—*two birds with one stone.*

I had been a miserable Christian—outwardly committed but inwardly joyless, crushed under the weight of performance. Hall's words felt like they were pulled from my own soul: "But I spent several years in *religion* before coming to

---

1. Wilcock, *The Message of Psalms*, 109.

embrace the freedom of Jesus' life."[2] That was me. But what's remarkable is this: it wasn't a new technique or therapy that set me free—*it was a revelation of God's grace*. In my case, the OCD and the striving weren't separate issues. They were two branches of the same root: a distorted, lifeless picture of God who was always frustrated and perpetually disappointed with me. When grace came in—real grace, the kind that flows from the heart of a Father who delights in his children—everything began to change.

AUGUSTINE'S FAVORITE

Some people spend their entire lives suffering under a suffocating weight of guilt, shame, or both. What a waste. What a tragedy. What a sadness. A guilty conscience cannot be neatly locked away, kept in a cozy container, and prevented from seeping into other areas of life. Guilt is all-pervasive, with poisonous tentacles that slowly and relentlessly wind their way into every pocket and corner of our existence. We end up living "restricted, loveless lives,"[3] driven by a miserable emptiness. Ironically, we do this while claiming to believe in the one who called himself "the life"[4] and said, "Whoever believes in me, as Scripture has said, rivers of living water will flow from within them."[5] In view of this tragic existential reality, there are three options:

1. Live with the guilt
2. Try and bury the guilt while lying to ourselves about its effects

---

2. Hall, *Grace Works*, 15.
3. Hall, *Grace Works*, 39.
4. John 14:6
5. John 7:38

3. Find a successful way to deal with the guilt and remove it from our lives

How can a guilty heart thrive? How can a guilty heart love deeply? How can a guilty heart avoid constant offense? How can a heart overwhelmed with guilty feelings focus on others—including God? Only option three leads to flourishing, enabling us to genuinely love and know others—including God—with our true, unhidden selves.

    The Bible is clear that trusting in the person, life, death, and resurrection of Jesus Christ is the only genuine way to deal with guilt. Every other attempt is a temporary distraction at best, a false remedy that placates only for a time. This is why Psalm 32 is so foundational—it focuses on God's rich, unearned, and wonderful forgiveness. It can only be received, never earned. Only a true and living trust in the saving work and person of Christ can bring a person to the place where they can say with confidence: "If God is for us, who can be against us?"[6] No wonder Psalm 32 was Augustine's favorite.[7] Peter Craigie writes: "Indeed, it is recorded that Ps 32 was Augustine's favorite psalm, that he read it frequently, and that before he died, he had its words inscribed on the wall by his sickbed, to be both exercised and comforted by them."[8]

    This is the first book in what I hope will become a long series, each one focusing on a single psalm. Different psalms highlight different themes. As Wilkerson and Boa write, "There are several kinds of psalms, and they express different feelings and circumstances. But the common theme is worship—God is worthy of all praise because of who He is, what He has done, and what He will do."[9] So what has he done? In

---

6. Rom 8:31
7. Waltner, *Psalms*, 172.
8. Craigie, *Psalms 1–50*, 268.
9. Wilkerson et al., *Talk Thru the Bible*, 153.

INTRODUCTION

Psalm 32, he has forgiven. Therefore, the focus of this book is to meditate on and celebrate God's wonderful forgiveness and the beautiful, life-changing impact it has on anyone who receives it. If any psalm bears the watermark of the cross, it is this one.

THE PENITENTIAL PSALMS

Psalm 32 is one of seven penitential psalms. The term "penitential" comes from the word "penitence," which refers to a feeling of deep regret or sorrow for wrongdoing, coupled with a desire to seek forgiveness and make amends. Thus, "penitential" describes anything related to or expressing repentance or remorse for sins or faults. Charles Spurgeon writes: "I would have you carefully study his penitential psalms, the language of which is ever full of weeping humility and earnest penitence."[10] I find the words "weeping humility" to be beautiful, poetic, and striking. The juxtaposition of an act (weeping) and a virtue (humility) is powerful: *a virtue possessed that now expresses itself emotionally in a person's life.*

Here are the seven penitential psalms:

Psalm 6	Prayer for God's Mercy
Psalm 32	The Blessedness of Forgiveness
Psalm 38	The Heavy Burden of Sin
Psalm 51	Confession and Forgiveness of Sin
Psalm 102	Prayer of an Overwhelmed Saint
Psalm 130	"My Soul Waits for the Lord"
Psalm 143	"Teach Me to Do Your Will"[11]

10. Spurgeon, "Confession of Sin," 252.

11. All of the short descriptions in this table are taken from Wilkerson and Boa, *Talk Thru the Bible*, 157–60.

Introduction

These seven psalms, a timeless gift to fallen humanity, offer profound and varied ways to pray the words of Jesus in the Lord's Prayer: "forgive us our sins, as we have forgiven those who sin against us."[12] The penitential psalms expand upon this petition, providing rich language to cry out to God for forgiveness when our hearts long to express more than a simple "forgive us our sins." We might view each psalm, although written approximately 1,000 years before the Lord's Prayer in Matthew 6, to be a footnote or commentary on it. The person who takes Spurgeon's advice to heart—who studies these seven—will be blessed and more easily find their way.

THE LORD'S PRAYER

Dietrich Bonhoeffer reminds us of the intimate connection between the Lord's Prayer and the Psalms. He quotes Martin Luther as saying: "It penetrates the Lord's Prayer and the Lord's Prayer penetrates it, so that it is possible to understand one on the basis of the other and bring them into joyful harmony."[13] Following this, Bonhoeffer himself writes:

> Thus the Lord's Prayer becomes the touchstone for whether we pray in the name of Jesus Christ or in your own name. It makes good sense, then, that the Psalter is often bound together in a single volume with the New Testament. It is the prayer of the Christian church. It belongs to the Lord's Prayer.[14]

While Psalm 32 serves as a footnote to the part of the Lord's Prayer that says, "forgive us our sins," the second part of the prayer—"as we have forgiven those who sin against us"—is not the focus of Psalm 32. While the psalm emphasizes the

---

12. Matt 6:12, New Living Translation.
13. Bonhoeffer, *Psalms*, 16.
14. Bonhoeffer, *Psalms*, 16.

joy and blessedness of receiving God's forgiveness, the Lord's Prayer invites us to reflect on the full scope of forgiveness as taught by Jesus. He completes this prayer by showing us the other side of the coin: *we are also called to forgive others as God has forgiven us.* In many ways, the life of discipleship is simple: *share with others what you have received freely from God.*

Paul underscores this truth in his letters. To the Christians in Colossae, a city in the Roman province of Asia Minor (modern-day Turkey), he writes: "Bear with each other and forgive one another if any of you has a grievance against someone. Forgive as the Lord forgave you."[15] Similarly, to the Ephesians, he exhorts: "Be kind and compassionate to one another, forgiving each other, just as in Christ God forgave you."[16] The message is clear: *as recipients of God's abundant mercy, we are called to share that mercy through the act of forgiveness.* I am not pretending that this is an easy word; it has not proven so for me. Yet we do not interpret God's Word according to our personal likes and dislikes. Scripture is not a blank canvas onto which we project our own meaning (a postmodern hermeneutic). Instead, we submit our likes and dislikes—all of the beauty and ugliness in human nature—to God's Word. It shapes us, not the other way around.

Returning to Psalm 32, the focus remains on God's willingness to forgive our sins. Consider this: who is more likely to forgive—someone drowning in guilt, unaware of God's love and forgiveness, or someone overwhelmed with thankfulness for having been forgiven by God? The answer is clear and echoed by our Lord: "Therefore, I tell you, her many sins have been forgiven—as her great love has shown. But whoever has been forgiven little loves little."[17]

---

15. Col 3:13
16. Eph 4:32
17. Luke 7:47

Introduction

Jesus teaches that the person who has been forgiven much will love much, likely because of the deep gratitude in their heart for God's mercy. They recognize that whatever wrongs have been done to them pale in comparison to the moral weight of their own sins against God. This profound awareness of grace transforms the heart, making forgiveness not only possible but a natural outflow of thankfulness to God. For this reason, spending an entire book meditating on God's willingness and eagerness to forgive our sins in Christ—as beautifully expressed in Psalm 32—is a worthy pursuit. It is anything but selfish. As his forgiveness sinks deeper into our conscious awareness, we become increasingly free to forgive others. In the end, we are all a bunch of ragamuffins in need of God's unearned mercy.

Blessed

Blessed is the one whose transgressions are forgiven, whose sins are covered. Blessed is the one whose sin the Lord does not count against them and in whose spirit is no deceit.

~Psalms 32:1–2

In certain parts of the United States, we say "bless you" when someone sneezes. Christians often part ways with the words, "Be blessed." And it's not uncommon to hear, "God bless you," whether in churches, emails, or moments of kindness. If we're honest, the word "blessed" has probably become overly familiar for many of us—so familiar, in fact, that its richness and theological significance are often diminished, reduced to something ordinary and commonplace. *Overuse can dull even the richest words.* That's why it's worth pausing to reflect on the simple fact that this word is the one used to open a psalm about forgiveness.

It seems obvious to me that if the God of Christianity truly exists and Psalm 32 is true, then our best shot at joy, peace, significance, and personal fulfillment lies in being blessed by him. Joy is one of the nine fruits of the Holy Spirit,[1]

---

1. Gal 5:22–23

who indwells the heart of every believer and desires to produce and cultivate those fruits both for God's glory and our good. The night before Jesus was crucified, he told his friends that he wanted their joy to be *complete*.[2] God genuinely desires to bless us, and to be blessed is to live under and in the gracious favor of the one who gives the blessing. Surely such a condition will affect every part of our lives. We will think better thoughts, enjoy deeper peace, find it easier to trust in the Lord and rule over anxiety and fear, love others more deeply in light of how we've been loved, experience healthier relationships, be more generous, and so on and so forth. To be blessed is to live in a state of divine favor, looked upon with delight by the one who matters most.

ARISTOTLE AND EUDAIMONIA

I have heard it said that among all of the works of philosophical ethics throughout Western history, Aristotle's *Nicomachean Ethics*—the first systematic treatment of Virtue Ethics—reigns supreme. In this book, he distinguishes between three types, or categories, of goods that human beings pursue. There are goods that are pursued only for the sake of something else. In other words, they are *instrumentally* good, not *intrinsically* good. This type of good, like money, is never desired for its own sake. Second, there are goods that are both instrumentally and intrinsically good. While they are good in themselves, they are still pursued for something greater. For Aristotle, honor, pleasure, intellect, and virtue are examples of this type of good. Then there is the final, ultimate good. It is an intrinsic good and is never pursued for the sake of something else (i.e., it is never instrumental). Aristotle identified happiness (i.e., eudaimonia) as this chief

---

2. John 15:11

good because it alone is that which "no one chooses for the sake of any of these nor indeed for the sake of anything else."[3]

While "happiness" appears in our English translations, the Greek word Aristotle used—*eudaimonia*—doesn't refer to our modern, Western idea of happiness as a fleeting emotion that can come and go multiple times in a single day. Rather, it is better translated as "flourishing" or "living well." It is more of a state of being than an emotional experience. It is this state, or condition, that Aristotle believed to be the ultimate good for human beings.

Aristotle is right that we desire happiness. We want to flourish, live well, and achieve what psychologist Erik Erickson identified as *ego integrity*. Ego integrity is a sense of wholeness and fulfillment that comes from accepting one's life as meaningful and coherent as one looks back. Those who embrace their past with acceptance experience a sense of wholeness and wisdom, while those who see their lives as wasted may fall into despair, experiencing bitterness and regret. We only get one chance at this thing called *life*, and no one wants to blow it. So how do we flourish? What does it mean to live well? How can a deep, permanent happiness be ours? Fortunately, Christianity has answers for all of these deep, existential questions.

While Aristotle is right that we desire to flourish, there are obvious differences between his views and what the Bible teaches. This should come as no surprise considering that Aristotle relied solely on reason and observation—*an autonomous approach*—while those inspired to write Scripture were guided by the perfect Holy Spirit. So while we can agree with Aristotle that we all desire happiness in the deepest part of our being, we as Christians do not exalt human happiness as the ultimate, final good. Rather, this blessed state is more

---

3. Aristotle, *Nicomachean Ethics*, 10.

of a byproduct. The ultimate good is God, and we are invited and commanded to glorify him in all that we are and do. As we live for his glory, we are blessed and satisfied with his goodness as a result. I've long been convinced that one of the most beautiful aspects of God's goodness is that his glory and our *eternal* good are never in conflict. Imagine the horror if we were forced to choose—either pursue what honors God or seek what is truly good for us. But that is not our predicament. In God's economy, his glory and our good are two sides of the same coin. Our deepest and most lasting good brings him glory, and his glorification always overflows in our good.

Returning to the first two verses, they pull back a curtain and reveal God's nature—*God is not a killjoy*. He is neither the enemy of our joy nor the antagonist in our story. As Paul writes, "If God is for us, who can be against us?"[4] Hidden within this single word that opens Psalm 32 is a portrait of God's heart as a Father. *Blessed* is a window into his very nature. This psalm is not about God rubbing our noses in sin but about him placing his hand gently under our chin, lifting our head until our eyes meet his—*he is the lifter of our heads*[5]—and setting us free from both sin and its crippling guilt. While a lion, he is also a lamb, a benevolent and patient Father who is "filled with compassion"[6] at the first sight of his beloved, yet filthy child. He is moved to "[run] to his son, [throw] his arms around him and [kiss] him."[7] God's heart flows downward, and thus his blessing awaits any soul that bows in humility, returns in confession, and seeks his grace.

---

4. Rom 8:31
5. Ps 3:3
6. Luke 15:20
7. Luke 15:20

We see this most clearly in the Parable of the Pharisee and the Tax Collector.[8]

But we might ask: *Is it selfish to desire God's blessing?* Is it morally wrong to desire my own good, especially in light of Bible verses like Philippians 2:3–4, which say: "Do nothing out of selfish ambition or vain conceit. Rather, in humility value others above yourselves, not looking to your own interests but each of you to the interests of the others." A major distinction must be made between *selfishness* and *self-interest*. Selfishness is putting one's own desires above the well-being of others, often disregarding their needs or rights, while self-interest involves pursuing what benefits oneself in a way that can still respect and consider the interests of others. While selfishness is condemned as sinful throughout the Bible, self-interest is not. As a matter of fact, God surprisingly appeals to self-interest throughout the Old and New Testaments. For example, Paul appeals to our natural inclination to seek our own good throughout 1 Corinthians 13, where Christlike love is celebrated and described. In 1 Corinthians 13:3, he reminds us that even if we give all we possess to the poor and endure great hardship, we *gain nothing* if love is not our motivation. God created us to desire our own good. To not desire our own good is not moral or spiritual maturity; rather, it is to be less than human and possibly out of reach of any rehabilitation. Desiring our own good is *not* selfish. The real question is: Where does that good ultimately lie? What is its source? Is there enough to share with others? How will I go about trying to secure that good? These are the questions that matter.

---

8. Luke 18:9–14

PSALM 32

"BLESSED" IN THE BIBLE

We've discussed that the word blessed carries deep significance, that all of us long to be happy, and that if Psalm 32 is true, our only real hope of flourishing lies in God. So, what does the word "blessed" actually mean? Anytime we ask a question like this as Christians, we must begin with the Bible. Most of the Old Testament was originally written in Hebrew while the New Testament was primarily written in Koine Greek. Because of this, it is always important not to simply read a word in its translated form (English, in this case) and assume that what comes to our 21st-century Western minds is exactly what the author intended in the original context. With that said, BibleHub.com explains:

> The Hebrew word for "blessed" is *ashrei*, which conveys a sense of happiness, contentment, and divine favor. In the biblical context, being blessed is not merely about material wealth or external circumstances but about a deep-seated joy and peace that comes from a right relationship with God. This word sets the tone for the entire psalm, emphasizing the spiritual prosperity and inner joy that come from experiencing God's forgiveness and grace.[9]

The part of this definition that stands out the most is "a deep-seated joy and peace that comes from right relationship with God."

When my Dad died several years ago, Mom promised me the Bible he had preached from. After about four years, she was ready to let it go, and I'm now reading through his Bible. It has been special and meaningful to see what he highlighted and underlined along with the notes he wrote in the margins. At the end of Psalm 32, Dad scribbled: "Joy comes from being right with God."

---

9. "Psalm 32: Study Guide," Bible Hub.

How true are these words! "Blessed" does not connote a superficial, fleeting emotional high. While emotions are a gift from God and a special (albeit complex) part of human nature—God himself experiences emotions[10]—they can quickly run amuck and be the source of pain and distress. "Blessed" refers to something far deeper than a fleeting emotion. It carries the sense of joyful flourishing. So while David says "blessed is the one," we could just as truly say, "How joyful is the one whose sins are forgiven!" It is a joy and peace rooted in a right relationship with God—one that remains intact, steady, and unshaken through the ups and downs of life. God desires this blessing, this joy, for every single person.

Psalm 32:1–2 serve as a general introduction to the psalm. Both verses begin with the word "blessed" which resembles the language found in the Beatitudes in Matthew 5 of the Sermon on the Mount. We might rewrite them as: "Happy are those who recognize that they are not righteous, and who know what to do about it."[11] Who is happy and content and fortunate? *The one whose sins are forgiven and no longer counted against them.* Ultimately, this psalm is one of thanksgiving for who God is—a forgiving God—and what he is willing to do.

THREE WORDS FOR SIN

While the NIV is the preferred translation for this book you have in your hands, it obscures the fact that three different

---

10. John 11:35, the shortest verse in the Bible—"Jesus wept"—is evidence enough that God himself not only feels, but feels deeply. Emotions were his idea, grounded in his own nature and instilled in human beings as an important part of what it means to be created imago Dei (i.e., in his image). Overly rationalist visions of what the imago Dei entails is probably due more to an Enlightenment-flavored anthropology than a close examination of Scripture.

11. Wilcock, *The Message of Psalms*, 109.

Hebrew words are used for sin in the first two verses. The New Revised Standard Version makes it more clear: "Happy are those whose *transgression* is forgiven, whose *sin* is covered. Happy are those to whom the Lord imputes no *iniquity*, and in whose spirit there is no deceit."[12] *Transgression. Sin. Iniquity.* Regarding these three terms, David Guzik with the Blue Letter Bible observes:

In these first two verses, David used three [Hebrew] words to describe sin.

- The idea behind *transgression* is crossing a line, defying authority.
- The idea behind *sin* is falling short of or missing a mark.
- The idea behind *iniquity* is of crookedness and distortion.

In the first two verses, David used three [Hebrew] terms to describe what God does to put away sin.

- The idea behind *forgiven* is the lifting of a burden or a debt.
- The idea behind *covered* is that of sacrificial blood covering sin.
- The idea behind *does not impute* is bookkeeping; it does not count against a person.[13]

Happy is the person who is forgiven. Happy is the person whose sins are covered. Happy is the person whose sins are not counted against them. One commentary states: "It is the relief of an enormous burden lifted, of a debt canceled, of a conscience at rest. Guilt is gone, warfare is ended, peace is enjoyed."[14]

---

12. Italics mine
13. Guzik, "Study Guide for Psalm 32."
14. MacDonald, *Believer's Bible Commentary*, Logos.

Interestingly, Paul quotes Psalm 32:1-2 in Romans 4 when he discusses the doctrine of justification by faith, emphasizing that righteousness is credited apart from works and is a gift of grace to those who believe. This is a great moment to mention that The Book of Psalms is the most quoted book in the New Testament. This is an important fact for Christians to consider in their daily walk with the Lord. If the people God used to write the New Testament drew more heavily from the Psalms than any other book, then we would be wise to give this book special attention as we seek to believe, love, worship, and obey God in all things.

THE BLESSED LIFE

Psalm 32:1-2 are not the only verses that begin with "Blessed" in reference to human beings. While we are called to praise, or bless, the Lord on numerous occasions (Psalm 66:20, 68:19, 72:18), the Psalms are also filled with "Blessed are you if..." statements. They are conditional statements that reveal the kinds of attitudes, orientations of the heart, and actions that God delights in.

- "**Blessed is the one** who does not walk in step with the wicked or stand in the way that sinners take or sit in the company of mockers" (Psalm 1:1).
- "Taste and see that the Lord is good; **blessed is the one** who takes refuge in him" (Psalm 34:8).
- "**Blessed is the one** who trusts in the Lord, who does not look to the proud, to those who turn aside to false gods" (Psalm 40:4).
- "**Blessed are those** who have regard for the weak; the Lord delivers them in times of trouble" (Psalm 41:1).

- "**Blessed are those** you choose and bring near to live in your courts! We are filled with the good things of your house, of your holy temple" (Psalm 65:4).
- "**Blessed are those** who dwell in your house; they are ever praising you. Blessed are those whose strength is in you, whose hearts are set on pilgrimage . . . Lord Almighty, **blessed is the one** who trusts in you" (Psalm 84:4–5, 12).
- "**Blessed are those** who have learned to acclaim you, who walk in the light of your presence, Lord" (Psalm 89:15).
- "**Blessed is the one** you discipline, Lord, the one you teach from your law" (Psalm 94:12).
- "**Blessed are those** who act justly, who always do what is right" (Psalm 106:3).
- "**Blessed are those** who fear the Lord, who find great delight in his commands" (Psalm 112:1).
- "**Blessed are those** whose ways are blameless, who walk according to the law of the Lord. **Blessed are those** who keep his statutes and seek him with all their heart" (Psalm 119:1–2).
- "**Blessed is the man** whose quiver is full of them. They will not be put to shame when they contend with their opponents in court" (Psalm 127:5).
- "**Blessed are all** who fear the Lord, who walk in obedience to him. You will eat the fruit of your labor; blessings and prosperity will be yours" (Psalm 128:1–2).
- "**Blessed is the people** of whom this is true; blessed is the people whose God is the Lord" (Psalm 144:15).
- "**Blessed are those** whose help is the God of Jacob, whose hope is in the Lord their God" (Psalm 146:5).

The Psalms make it unmistakably clear that God wants to bless you and me. He desires good for his people. Blessed if you do this. Blessed if you don't do that. Blessed if you have this. The list goes on. What stands out is not just that God wants to bless us, but that he longs for our blessing so deeply that he goes to great lengths to reveal what is required. He doesn't keep his cards close, so to speak. He is vulnerable and transparent so that we may know what he wants and how to position ourselves to receive his fullness.

Returning to Psalm 32, the focus is undeniably on forgiveness. These first two verses set the stage for the entire psalm by providing a bird's eye view of what David will recount and celebrate in the words that follow. Truly, few things are more precious and transforming than God's willingness to forgive us in Christ. His hands and heart are wide open.

AN EXISTENTIAL CONDITION

The first two verses do not merely promise forgiveness unconditionally. An important existential condition must be satisfied to receive and enjoy this forgiveness: *living honestly before God*. While the first two verses celebrate the richness and depth of God's forgiveness, verse two ends with: "and in whose spirit is no deceit." Bible scholar Bruce Waltke writes: "'In one's spirit is no deceit' (i.e., a sincere confession) is the fundamental condition for God's grace to pervade and cleanse the guilty conscience."[15] In other words, God's mercy is applied and enjoyed only when we live honestly before God, confessing sins as the Holy Spirit sheds light, and living in a constant and deep dependence on God's grace to grow and mature. You and I don't have to have it all together.

---

15. Waltke, "Psalms 1–41."

A *spirit of deceit* refers to an inner, continual disposition characterized by a refusal to admit sin and engage in conversations with the Lord about that sin. One insulates oneself from the uncomfortable, nudging convictions of the Holy Spirit. It becomes a lifestyle, a way of being. One lives in denial. David wants us to avoid this path, having trod it at some point in his past. The simple words, "and in whose spirit is no deceit," reveal that if you desire God's forgiveness and want to enjoy his blessing, then you must be honest with the Lord. You must be an open book with the Lord, not deceiving yourself with lies about your moral innocence. Simply stated, confession is required. Pastor Paul Tripp writes: "confession of sin isn't a prelude to judgment; confession of sin is a way to enter into the grace of God's forgiveness."[16] God's mercy is freely given through Christ when we do not pretend to be righteous—right before God—based on our efforts. The book of Romans and the entire New Testament are clear that you can't do enough good or avoid enough evil to earn your way into good standing with God.

READING THROUGH THE LENS OF CHRIST

While this would be a great place to conclude the chapter, I want to make one more important hermeneutical observation that will play a key role in this book. Hermeneutics is:

> The discipline that studies the principles and theories of how texts ought to be interpreted, particularly sacred texts such as the Scriptures. Hermeneutics also concerns itself with understanding the unique roles and relationships between the author, the text and the original or subsequent readers.[17]

---

16. Tripp, "Psalm 32: The Blessing of Confession and Forgiveness."
17. Grenz et al., *Pocket Dictionary of Theological Terms*, 59.

Hermeneutically, it is crucial to interpret Psalm 32 (as well as any other psalm) through the lens of the life, teachings, death, and resurrection of Jesus Christ. Pastor, theologian, and martyr Dietrich Bonhoeffer is among the best at reminding us to remain Christocentric when reading any passage of the Bible, especially when addressing topics like forgiveness and righteousness. In one place Bonhoeffer writes: "We want to meet Christ in his word."[18] In another place, he writes: "The Psalms are given to us to this end, that we may learn to pray them in the name of Jesus Christ."[19] Regarding Bonhoeffer's Christocentric approach, Walter Brueggemann of Columbia Theological Seminary writes: "The daily practice of praying the Psalms thus cannot be simply a comfortable devotional exercise. Rather, it is the reframing of all of life toward the rule of Christ."[20] One of the clearest examples of where a Christocentric focus is needed is in the final words of Psalm 32: "Rejoice in the Lord and be glad, you righteous. . ." Who are the righteous? To be righteous in Christ means being made right with God through faith in Jesus Christ, not by our own works. Through his perfect life, death, and resurrection, Christ secures the forgiveness of sins for believers, and his righteousness is credited to them.[21] This gift of righteousness establishes peace with God and the assurance of being justified in his sight (Romans 5:1). Truly, we are saved from our sins *by grace* and *through faith—sola gratia, sola fide!*[22]

18. Bonhoeffer, *Meditating on the Word*, 32.

19. Bonhoeffer, *Psalms*, 15.

20. Walter Brueggemann, *Introduction to Psalms: The Prayer Book of the Bible*, 6.

21. 2 Cor 5:21; Rom 3:22

22. The five solas—sola scriptura (Scripture alone), sola fide (faith alone), sola gratia (grace alone), solus Christus (Christ alone), and soli Deo gloria (to the glory of God alone)—were foundational principles of the Reformation, emphasizing salvation through faith in Christ by grace as revealed in Scripture, all for God's glory. C. Stephen Evans writes of *sola fide* that it "refers to the

Psalm 32

As we explore Psalm 32 together, Christ and his redemptive work must remain central as we meditate on every word, phrase, and sentence.

WHY GOD NOT FORGETTING OUR SIN IS A GOOD THING

There is one more point worth exploring. I have heard before that when God forgives, he casts our sins into a sea of forgetfulness. At face value, this promises immense comfort to the person that cannot find a way to forgive themselves for past deeds. Language like "sea of forgetfulness" is probably based on verses like Micah 7:19: "You will again have compassion on us; you will tread our sins underfoot and hurl all our iniquities into the depths of the sea." This paired with other Bible verses seems to paint a picture of God, who is otherwise omniscient, choosing to delete our sins from his memory. For example, God speaks in Jeremiah 31:34: "For I will forgive their wickedness and will remember their sins no more." Isaiah 43:25 reads: "I, even I, am he who blots out your transgressions, for my own sake, and remembers your sins no more." Hebrews 8:12 states, "For I will forgive their wickedness and will remember their sins no more." The message seems to be clear: *God not only forgives but forgets.* But what does "forget" really mean? Without much reflection, we might assume that this means a type of literal amnesia.

But does this make sense?

And is it even desirable?

Reformation doctrine that salvation is completely the result of faith and is in no way the outcome of good works." See Evans, *Pocket Dictionary of Apologetics & Philosophy of Religion*, 109.

In my view, the answer is *no* on both accounts. If God were to literally forget our sins, as in erasing them from his memory in the way that humans forget trivial details, this would introduce serious theological problems. Pastor H.P. McCracken writes: "God's 'forgetting' cannot be literal memory loss, equivalent to my forgetting math formulas from high school, because this contradicts what the Bible teaches about God's omniscience, His total and perfect knowledge."[23] God is omniscient—he knows all things, past, present, and future. For him to truly forget something in the way we do would mean that there is something outside of his knowledge, which contradicts his very nature. *Moreover, would it really be comforting to serve a God who no longer remembers key moments of our own story?* Many of us still wrestle with the consequences of past sins, seeking healing in relationships or struggling to embrace his grace. If God had no recollection of our failures, how could he guide us through the restoration process? How could he remind us of his faithfulness in bringing us out of darkness and into the light?

Instead, the biblical language of God "remembering no more" must be understood in a *relational* sense rather than a *cognitive* one. When Scripture says God does not remember our sins, it means he no longer holds them against us. They no longer define our standing before him. This is the essence of forgiveness—God does not treat us according to our transgressions, nor does he allow them to hinder our communion with him. Psalm 32:2 affirms this truth: "Blessed is the one whose sin the Lord does not count against them . . ." The emphasis is not on divine amnesia but on the complete removal of guilt and condemnation.

In reality, we need a God who remembers, not to condemn, but to redeem. So often, he uses the memory of our

---

23. McCracken, "Isaiah 43:25."

past failures to shape us into people of greater wisdom, humility, and compassion. Many who have sinned grievously and been forgiven find themselves called into some type of ministry that speaks directly to those struggling in similar ways. How often does God use our wounds—many of which we inflicted upon ourselves through sinful actions—to comfort others with the comfort we have received (2 Cor. 1:3–4)? *A God who forgets in the way we do would not be able to transform our brokenness for his glory.*

This is why Romans 8:28 rings true: "And we know that in all things God works for the good of those who love him, who have been called according to his purpose." Our past sins, once confessed and forgiven, are not deleted from history but woven into a greater redemptive story. Augustine, one of the greatest theologians in church history, writes: "For the Omnipotent God, whom even the heathen acknowledge as the Supreme Power over all, would not allow any evil in his works, unless in his omnipotence and goodness, as the Supreme Good, he is able to bring forth good out of evil."[24] The comfort of divine forgiveness is not that God loses track of our failures but that he remembers them in a way that leads to restoration, renewal, and ultimately, our joy in him.

The sting is gone.

There is no condemnation for those in Christ,[25] so we can be assured that whatever he remembers, he graciously remembers for our good and his glory.

---

24. Augustine, *Handbook on Faith, Hope, and Love.*
25. Rom 8:1

Heavy

When I kept silent, my bones wasted away through my groaning all day long. For day and night your hand was heavy on me; my strength was sapped as in the heat of summer.

~Psalm 32:3-4

It has rightly been noted that "one of the marks of the integrity of Scripture [is] that the low points as well as the triumphs of its principal characters are described."[1] Many believe that David is reflecting on his transgression with Bathsheba in Psalm 32, even though he does not mention it explicitly. It does seem to fit considering that there was a delay between David's sins and his repentance. The burden of his unconfessed sin—the adultery with Bathsheba[2] and the arranged death of her husband Uriah[3]—weighed heavily upon him. It wasn't until the prophet Nathan confronted him with a parable[4] that David acknowledged his wrongdoing and sought God's forgiveness. If this is the case, then Psalm

---

1. Radmacher et al., *The Nelson Study Bible: New King James Version*, Ps. 32. Logos.
2. 2 Sam 11:2-4
3. 2 Sam 11:14-17
4. 2 Sam 12:1-7

Psalm 32

32 is a sibling to Psalm 51, another of the seven penitential psalms. Both have been referred to as "confessional giants."[5]

If they are referencing the same event in David's life, some suggest that Psalm 51 and Psalm 32 reflect different stages of his experience. Psalm 51 captures his immediate response to sin and brokenness, while Psalm 32 serves as a later, more reflective meditation on the pain of delayed repentance and the joy of forgiveness. This might explain the upbeat mood of the psalm. Tremper Longman III writes: "Traditionally, Psalm 32 has been treated as a penitential psalm (along with Pss 6; 38; 51; 102; 130; 133). The tone of the song is not sorrowful, however, because this prayer was uttered in the aftermath of God's forgiveness."[6] Psalm 51 conveys the raw, broken, and desperate cry of a soul seeking mercy, whereas Psalm 32 offers a calmer, seasoned reflection after the pangs of guilt have subsided. Together, they provide a fuller picture of repentance and restoration, moving from anguish to peace—*a peace only found in Christ*. While we do not know for certain, this potential background sheds light on the emotional and spiritual struggle David describes.

While I will say more about this when we reach verse 6, it should not go unnoticed that David is praying. He is having a conversation with God while at the same time offering instruction to the reader/listener. It is a prayer with a didactic tone, explaining why this psalm is also considered a *wisdom psalm*. This is not merely David remembering; it is David remembering in the mode of prayer. We see this in the words, "For day and night your hand was heavy on me." David uses a second-person singular pronoun when referring to God—"your"—rather than speaking about God

---

5. MacArthur Jr., *The MacArthur Study Bible*, 769.
6. Longman III, *Psalms: An Introduction and Commentary*, 163.

in the third person (he or him). Thus, David is recounting an unrepentant time in a prayerful, even worshipful manner.

DAVID GETS PERSONAL

It is in verse three where the Psalm shifts—*When I kept silent*. It is a jolting, hard pivot from a general introduction about forgiveness to David recounting a time when he chose not to receive and enjoy God's forgiveness. He was closed off. You can attempt to pour water into a bucket all day, but nothing can enter if the lid is still on. There was a lid on David's heart; he was barricaded. God's life could not reach him. While Psalm 32 begins with a general reflection on the joy inherent in knowing God's unearned and undeserved forgiveness, David now plunges into his past; he gets personal. As one commentary explains, "'I kept silent' signifies active, intentional silence."[7] Here, David remembers a time when he locked God out and kept him at a distance. His heart was hard. He refused, like we often do, to soften and confess to God: "I was wrong. I have sinned. I am so sorry."

To resist God is always a recipe for both internal turmoil and external chaos. Refusing to break down and repent can result in increased anxiety, a compassionless heart, depression, and an overall inability to enjoy God's gifts all around us.[8] When we're not right with God and refuse to come clean, it can feel like a cloud hangs overhead, casting a shadow even on the good things that would normally bring us joy. Everything becomes lifeless and without color until the relationship is repaired. Eventually, we must either repent or

---

7. Waltke et al., *The Psalms as Christian Lament*, 113.
8. I'm not suggesting that all experiences of depression stem from sin. Such a claim cannot be supported by Scripture and should never be taught. At the same time, I do believe that depression can, at times, result from living in unrepentant sin.

walk away from God altogether—his gaze leaves no room for a genuine third option. Anything else is mere pretending which will always lead to a withered soul.

GOD WILL MAKE US MISERABLE

The *heavy hand* of God suggests a remarkably uncomfortable and unsettling truth: *God will make us miserable to make us happy*. Of course, his goal is not to simply make us happy; ultimately, he seeks to glorify himself which also turns out to be for our good. But he is not opposed to our happiness. *God wants us to live deeply satisfied with him and the good things he has shared with us*. David Guzik writes:

> David's dryness and misery were actually a good thing. They demonstrated that he was in fact a son of God, and that the covenant God would not allow him to remain comfortable in habitual or unconfessed sin. One who feels no misery or dryness in such a state has far greater concerns for time and eternity.[9]

After writing that the dryness and misery were actually a good thing, Guzik claims that these two experiences "demonstrated that he was in fact a son of God." What does he mean? Proverbs 3:11–12 states: "My son, do not despise the Lord's discipline, and do not resent his rebuke, because the Lord disciplines those he loves, as a father the son he delights in." The same message is found in the New Testament. In Hebrews 12:5–6, the writer refers to these words in Proverbs and then goes on to write:

> Endure hardship as discipline; God is treating you as his children. For what children are not disciplined by their father? If you are not disciplined— and everyone undergoes discipline—then you are

---

9. Guzik, "Study Guide for Psalm 32."

> not legitimate, not true sons and daughters at all. Moreover, we have all had human fathers who disciplined us and we respected them for it. How much more should we submit to the Father of spirits and live! They disciplined us for a little while as they thought best; but God disciplines us for our good, in order that we may share in his holiness. No discipline seems pleasant at the time, but painful. Later on, however, it produces a harvest of righteousness and peace for those who have been trained by it.[10]

The message is unmistakable: *if you are a child of God through faith in the person and work of Christ, then God loves you too much to remain silent when sin takes root in your life.* He will discipline you because you are his child. As a father, I do not discipline children I do not know—they are strangers to me. But it's different with my own three. My wife and I discipline our children because we love them and recognize that certain attitudes and actions today can affect them negatively in the future. Because we want what's best for them, we cannot simply stand by. *Love requires more.*

We cannot easily escape the Father's reach. His love is truly relentless—a reality that mere human reason cannot fully grasp. For David, the dryness and misery he experienced were, in fact, good because they came from God. God is jealous, saying to Moses: "For I, the Lord your God, am a jealous God." For most of us, we have met with only twisted, broken, and sin-oriented expressions of jealousy. But this is not true of God's jealousy. It burns with a white-hot love. He knows that only he can satisfy our hearts, and will jealousy fight and sing and dance to win our hearts every time we try and get away. Even when he gives us some slack and lets us run, he remains close. In what is a mystery, a person can be far from God without God being far from them.

---

10. Heb 12:7–11

When we refuse to acknowledge, confess, and turn from our sins—an intentional act of defiance where God is pushed away in one or more areas of our lives—God will apply his heavy hand, press it down on us, and drain all of our strength. We grow weary of hiding, of holding back, of not bearing our soul. We might even find it next to impossible to experience joy in anyone or anything else. Warren Wiersbe writes: "The longer you wait, the more miserable you will be, as you can see in David's experience."[11] *God is unrelenting—even annoyingly so—in his extravagant mercy.* He will allow us to stay in the field for an indefinite period of time feeding the dirty pigs and eating their food until we finally come to the point that we can pray: "I will set out and go back to my father and say to him: 'Father, I have sinned against heaven and against you. I am no longer worthy to be called your son; make me like one of your hired servants.'"[12]

David resisted God's conviction and call to repent. He remained impenetrable for a time. He planted his feet and dug in his heels *against* God. Someone would eventually budge, but David's pride caused him to think that it would be God, not himself, and that he would somehow achieve what Jacob could not—*win at wrestling with God.*[13] Of course, to "win" would be to lose, and to lose would be to win. Christ communicates this beautiful paradox: "Whoever wants to be my disciple must deny themselves and take up their cross and follow me. For whoever wants to save their life will lose it, but whoever loses their life for me and for the gospel will save it."[14]

The moment of breaking is truly one of the sweetest experiences available to a human being. The heavy hand is

---

11. Wiersbe, *With the Word Bible Commentary*, Ps 32.
12. Luke 15:18–19
13. Gen 32:22–32
14. Mark 8:34–35

lifted, the weight removed, the pressure eased. God comes close again (as if he was ever far away). His voice can be heard again. As David writes elsewhere: "My sacrifice, O God, is a broken spirit; a broken and contrite heart you, God, will not despise."[15] In Anthem, artist Leonard Cohen sings: "Ring the bells that still can ring, forget your perfect offering. There is a crack, a crack in everything. That's how the light gets in."[16] God breaks the heart so that he can enter it once more.

God always acts with eternity in mind, so making us miserable for a time is easy work for him. *It would break his heart more to not break ours.* He will do it. He will always do it. He is never a slave to the moment, always seeing the full picture even while he deals with us in the moment. If you have trusted in the person and work of Christ, he will not leave you alone. This is good news. Worship him for it. He is the great gadfly, putting Socrates to shame.[17] He will buzz, sting, and keep you off balance until you fall on your knees.

Until you break.

Until you give up.

THE BEAUTIFUL, HEAVY HAND OF GOD

Does the idea of God's heavy hand bother you? If so, then I encourage you to sit with this truth rather than run from it. Take a moment to reflect. Your discomfort could point to a number of things:

15. Ps 51:17
16. Cohen, "Anthem."
17. Socrates was called the "gadfly" because, like a gadfly that constantly stings a horse to keep it awake and moving, he provoked the people of Athens with challenging questions to awaken them from intellectual complacency and stir them to pursue truth and virtue. This metaphor appears in Plato's *Apology*.

- A distorted or shallow theology of God
- Painful experiences with a father figure that continue to shade your view of God
- Pride that resists the notion of divine discipline
- A cultural view of love that excludes correction

Regarding the first item in the list, 20th century pastor and author A.W. Tozer writes what has long been one of my favorite quotes: "What comes into our minds when we think about God is the most important thing about us ... the most portentous fact about any man is not what he at a given time may say or do, but what he in his deep heart conceives God to be like."[18] What do you believe about God–or not believe— that would prevent you from recognizing the heavy hand as a part of the Christian experience? God loves us too much and is too committed to our *eternal* good to leave us in the mud, so he applies his heavy hand in pursuit of our hearts. He is rightly named *The Hound of Heaven* in Francis Thompson's 19th-century poem:

> I fled Him, down the nights and down the days;
> I fled Him, down the arches of the years;
> I fled Him, down the labyrinthine ways
> Of my own mind; and in the mist of tears
> I hid from Him, and under running laughter.
> Up vistaed hopes I sped;
> And shot, precipitated,
> Adown Titanic glooms of chasmèd fears,
> From those strong Feet that followed, followed after.
> But with unhurrying chase,
> And unperturbèd pace,
> Deliberate speed, majestic instancy,
> They beat—and a Voice beat
> More instant than the Feet—

---

18. Tozer, *The Knowledge of the Holy*, 9.

"All things betray thee, who betrayest Me."[19]

The purpose of being confronted with the truth—or confronting someone else with it—is always freedom. Only the truth sets free, and only unbound hearts can truly enter into genuine, life-giving relationships with each other. This is true of our relationship with God and people. God presses his heavy hand—squishing, smashing, and squeezing our lives—so that we eventually break. God is not afraid of pain. Sometimes, the wisest thing we can do is stop overthinking and simply surrender.

In God's economy, pain always has a purpose. We must choose to not waste it although this is hard to do initially. The painful, uncomfortable pressure is not the end, but only the means to another end. When the end is achieved, the pain—the inexplicable divine pressure—can be removed. The relationship is restored. The lines of communication are open.

But not yet—we haven't made it that far into the psalm. Verses three and four are where David recalls the pressure, the pain, the heartache, the coldness, and the aloofness. It was his fault. Sinning is one thing, but refusing to own it is another. The latter might be worse. A dam now blocked the living waters from David's soul. He was withering. Yet God would not let him off the hook, so to speak. What did God do instead?

He turned up the pressure.

He increased David's discomfort.

He let David's heart become a barren wasteland.

---

19. Thompson, "The Hound of Heaven."

Psalm 32

God breaks us so that he can mend us. He makes us miserable so that we can be happy . . . *in him*. As the prophet Hosea knew and expressed: "Come, let us return to the Lord. He has torn us to pieces but he will heal us; he has injured us but he will bind up our wounds."[20] Always attributing discomfort to Satan may blind us to the refining work of God. If you feel God's heavy hand, you may not feel much else—until you break. So break! Fall on the mercy of God that flows from the cross and delight in being fully dependent on him. If Scripture is true, there is no other path to real joy.

---

20. Hos 6:1

Break

Then I acknowledged my sin to you and did not cover up my iniquity. I said, "I will confess my transgressions to the Lord." And you forgave the guilt of my sin.

~Psalm 32:5

We are all familiar with the phrases, "That's the straw that broke the camel's back," "He is at his breaking point," or "I just can't take much more." These expressions are never used positively. They signal that a person is overwhelmed, unable to handle much more. They are on the brink of collapse, and one more piece of bad news or another bad turn might just be the nail in the coffin.

We all face moments in life when we feel overwhelmed, as though the proverbial last straw might finally break our back. Christians are not exempt from these feelings; we, too, can be overwhelmed. And then, to make matters worse, we add guilt to the equation—guilt for feeling overwhelmed—because surely this must mean we're not trusting God enough. Any human moment of weakness can quickly become, in our minds, an indictment against our spirituality.

We might not like the idea that God permits pain and difficulty—and that's putting it nicely—but no one can read the Bible and come away with a different conclusion. He is the God who didn't stop Cain from murdering Abel, who destroyed most of the human race with a flood, who sent an evil spirit to torment Saul, who allowed his people to serve as slaves in Egypt for 400 years, who remained silent for nearly 400 years before John the Baptist arrived on the scene, and who allowed his own Son to die a brutal death.

If restoring fellowship with him requires it, God will bring us to a breaking point. He will apply internal pressure, permit painful confusion, remove every crumb of peace and joy, arrange unsettling circumstances, and even allow the world around us to crumble—all with the intent of awakening us.

Sometimes, what we need most is to break—nothing more, nothing less. Nothing will be right until we do. David reached his breaking point through God's heavy hand and a deep spiritual dryness—and he finally broke. He could not resist any longer. Enough was enough. His unrepentant heart was proving to costly. Like David, we can keep stumbling forward under the life-sucking weight of our sin or we can fall to our knees and surrender. In the spiritual life, surrender is not defeat; it is the beginning of freedom and the path to true joy.

But first we must break.

We must give in.

We must allow the heavy hand to win.

While verse 3 marks a shift in the psalm from general reflection to personal confession, it is verse 5 that opens the way for the return of God's goodness that unfolds in the rest of the psalm. Here we encounter the sweet words God wants to hear: "I acknowledged my sin" and "I will confess." This is the moment in the psalm when the dam breaks and the waters are released.

Life can start again.

Heart can touch heart.

God's love can now color David's life once more.

BROKEN, NOT CRUSHED

Jesus said something striking to the religious leaders of his day: "Anyone who falls on this stone will be broken to pieces; anyone on whom it falls will be crushed." Let's not overcomplicate his words—they serve as both a warning and an invitation. Likely building on Psalm 118:22, Jesus is teaching that it is far better to fall on the rock in surrender and be broken than to have the rock fall on us in judgment and be crushed. Who besides Jesus can say such a harsh word while simultaneously lacing it with immense hope?

His words leave us with an unavoidable choice. When something is broken, it can be put back together. The pieces can be reassembled, sometimes even making the item stronger than it was before. But when an item is crushed, all that remains is dust or powder. It's gone—nothing is left that can be reassembled.

There's another important distinction to consider: a person doesn't choose for something to fall on them. When something is falling, our instinct is to move quickly out of the way. No one willingly stands still, waiting to be crushed. But falling, on the other hand, is often a deliberate choice. I fall onto a mattress when I'm tired. I dive into a stream or lake to enjoy the cool water. I fall to the ground to let my child feel the thrill of tackling me. Athletes in most sports can be seen falling to their knees—or even on their faces—when overwhelmed with emotion after an important, even improbable, victory. While we don't choose to be crushed, we often choose, in many circumstances, to fall.

There are two obvious differences between falling and being crushed: (1) something that is broken can be put back together, and (2) we can choose to fall and be broken. Both points are crucial for understanding the meaning of the verse we are reflecting on in this chapter. They remind us that Jesus invites us to choose: to fall on the rock and be broken—to repent and be restored—or to remain silent in pride and be crushed under the weight of sin. What we have in verse 5 is David finally choosing to fall on the rock and be broken. Elsewhere David prays, "Have mercy on me, Lord; heal me, for I have sinned against you."[1] These are the words that God waits to hear. These are the words that bring him near. Only then can the one who heals—Jehovah Rapha—make whole. He once said to Moses and the people: "For I am the Lord, who heals you."[2] That has never changed, nor will it.

This is the choice David had to make—but unfortunately, he did not make it quickly. We all sin, but a true test of the heart and our walk with the Lord is how long it takes us to repent when the Holy Spirit is convicting us of sin. We grieve the Holy Spirit and thereby are grieved; he is in every believer. To fall on the rock is to do exactly what David wrote: "Then I acknowledged my sin to you and did not cover up my iniquity." Confessing our sin is a humble step requiring that we refuse to hide any part of ourselves. While God will resist the proud, he runs to brokenness.

---

1. Ps 41:4
2. Ex 15:26

Of course, the idea of us hiding anything from God is almost comical—as if a human being could ever truly hide anything from an omniscient God. He knows all things. When we hide, we are not concealing anything from God but shielding our own conscious awareness from the truth he has always known. In other words, we cannot hide from God. What we are doing—foolishly—is hiding from reality, from truth, and even from ourselves. A person who is not at peace with God cannot be at peace with themselves. The latter is the fruit of the former. How could one resist who Isaiah calls the "Prince of Peace"[3] and yet possess peace apart from its source?

It must be admitted that we are sometimes moderately successful at hiding. Sinful acts and the guilt that follows can slide into our subconscious until we begin to think that we've moved on and that the sin is no longer affecting us. Yet there they are, quietly adding to the pile of emotional and spiritual baggage that actively works against our experience and expression of God's goodness. When we "hide" from God, we deceive only ourselves, pretending that he doesn't see what he has seen all along.

NOT ONLY THE SIN, BUT THE GUILT

After David tells us that he finally acknowledged his sin and confessed it to God, he writes something interesting at the end of verse 5: "And you forgave the guilt of my sin." Why doesn't David simply write, "And you forgave my sin"? Regarding this intriguing phrase, other translations state:

- "and thou forgavest the iniquity of my sin" (King James Version)

---

3. Isa 9:6

- "and you forgave the iniquity of my sin" (English Standard Version)
- "and You forgave the guilt of my sin" (New American Standard Bible)
- "and you forgave the guilt of my sin" (New Revised Standard Version)
- "and you forgave all my sins" (Good News Bible)
- "And you forgave me! All my guilt is gone" (New Living Translation)

We need to pause here and clarify what is meant by "guilt." Grenz and Smith write, "Guilt can be described either as an objective moral concept or as a subjective feeling."[4] In this context, guilt can refer to either an objective guilt before God—having sinned and now standing guilty in a moral and legal sense—or a subjective feeling of guilt. Most of these translations suggest that David is likely referring to guilt in the legal sense, much like a criminal being declared guilty in a court of law. That same criminal may or may not feel guilty in an emotional or psychological sense. This distinction is important.

We now need to ask ourselves: what kind of guilt is David referring to at the end of verse 5? Initially, it's important to recognize that the answer is likely both. When we consider the language and overall tone of Psalm 32, there is no compelling reason to adopt a rigid either/or approach; it seems more fitting to see this as a both/and. After all, David has already described his bones wasting away, groaning all day long, feeling the weight of God's heavy hand, and having his strength drained as in the heat of summer. These are vivid, subjective expressions of physical, emotional, and spiritual anguish. It seems safe to conclude that he felt guilt at a very

---

4. Grenz et al., *Pocket Dictionary of Ethics*, 48.

deep level—and that this internal experience was likely one of the primary ways God's heavy hand was made manifest.

That said, I believe the words at the end of verse 5 probably refer more to David's objective guilt before God. He has sinned and stands guilty, much like a criminal in a court of law stands guilty before a judge. So when David speaks of God forgiving "the guilt of his sin," the objective meaning is that David no longer stands condemned before God. He is forgiven and no longer charged with wrongdoing. He is free to know and enjoy God once more. Unconfessed sin no longer stands in the way.

While it is likely that David was referring to guilt in this objective sense, I want to discuss the importance of God working in the human heart after repentance to remove guilt in the subjective sense. A person cannot truly move on with God unless they receive emotional and spiritual relief. Freedom in the human heart depends on it.

Regarding guilt in the subjective sense, it is an emotional burden that weighs heavily on the heart and mind. Psychology Today describes it as "aversive" and notes that "people may feel guilt for a variety of reasons, including acts they have committed (or think they committed), a failure to do something they should have done, or thoughts they believe are morally wrong."[5] While guilt is considered a self-conscious emotion—like shame, embarrassment, and pride—it can play a significant role in the life of a Christian, as we see in David's story.

God not only forgave David's guilt in the objective sense, but he also removed the overwhelming feelings of guilt from David's heart. This explains, in part, the joyful and celebratory tone in Psalm 32. The Contemporary English Version (CEV) offers a particularly helpful rendering: "Then

---

5. "Guilt," *Psychology Today*.

you forgave me and took away my guilt." The full verse reads: "So I confessed my sins and told them all to you. I said, 'I'll tell the Lord each one of my sins.' Then you forgave me and took away my guilt. Selah." I appreciate the CEV's wording because of the clear distinction between the two types of guilt. While "forgave me" implicitly refers to the objective guilt that God took care of in the death and resurrection of Jesus Christ, the words "took away my guilt" seem to point toward guilt in the subjective sense. In Christ, God's forgiveness addresses both, which is necessary if we are not only to avoid condemnation, but also flourish as sons and daughters of God. Merely escaping punishment has never been God's end game. The forgiveness we have in Christ results in our being declared "Not guilty" before God—justified in his sight—and this declaration is always, both temporally and logically, a prerequisite for the subjective experience of guilt to be addressed in the human heart.

The removal of the subjective feeling of guilt in the human heart is utterly dependent on God first forgiving a person of their sins and removing the guilt in an objective, legal sense. In my Dad's Bible, which he studied and preached from, he wrote right below Psalm 32:5: "not just the sin—the guilt."

There is a clear logical order at work here: God forgives a person, and only then can the person's subjectively experienced guilt be rightly addressed. Any attempt to remove guilt experienced in human consciousness is misguided—even harmful—without God's forgiveness. The reason is simple: if one still stands guilty before God, then trying to remove subjective feelings of guilt is ultimately futile, because even if one succeeds to some degree, they remain objectively guilty before a holy God. The root still remains. To try to remove guilt—whether your own or someone else's—apart from the cross and repentance is ultimately deceptive. It prevents the one burdened with guilt from taking the only step that can truly bring relief: *confessing sin to God*. All other attempts are stolen—an attempt to grasp something that cannot truly be possessed apart from heartfelt confession. It is crucial that pastors and lay leaders in the church remember this as they minister. Do not rush to remove guilt; you might be working against God unless the person is ready to fall on the rock, be broken, and turn from their sin.

Only when God forgives us is there moral and spiritual authority to forgive ourselves and leave the guilt behind. Trying to get rid of guilty feelings apart from God is simply another form of rebellion—yet another attempt to live without him. It is an attempt to heal the heart while resisting the very Creator who offers true healing. God's forgiveness of sin is the only rightful foundation for the removal of guilt. Simply stated, we can forgive ourselves because God has forgiven us. We can let go of guilty feelings because God has forgiven us. Self-forgiveness is empty and vacuous if God has not first forgiven us. It is only God's forgiveness that grants us the moral and spiritual authority to forgive ourselves and leave our guilty feelings behind.

A CLEAN CONSCIENCE: *THE GIFT OF ALL GIFTS*

Thomas A. Kempis writes: "No man rejoiceth securely, unless he hath within him the testimony of a good conscience."[6] What is more precious than a clear conscience? I would say that you cannot put a price tag on one, but you can: *the death and resurrection of Jesus Christ*. One doesn't have to look far to find someone whose entire life—their every waking thought and act—is shaped by the residue of guilt that lingers from past deeds. At first, feelings of guilt can be piercingly hot, but after some time, they subside. We begin

---

6. Kempis, *The Imitation of Christ*, 61.

thinking that the guilt is gone, but it isn't—*guilt must be dealt with*. It doesn't simply disappear. Instead, it slips into a dark corner of our psyche, sets up camp, and slowly eats away at everything good—like termites devouring wood. When not addressed and *properly* removed, subjective feelings of guilt burrow deep into the soul with roots that cannot be extracted by mere human effort. When this occurs, the guilt becomes increasingly pervasive and comprehensive in its consumption of the soul. Only in Christ does hope remain. Only he is powerful enough to deal with sin and its tragic effects.

If sin is the legal barrier between a holy God and a sinful person (objective guilt), experienced guilt is the subjective, psychological barrier. The guilt must go if the heart is to be free to enjoy friendship with God. A guilt-ridden heart cannot commune. Think of a man who has cheated on his wife but has refused to tell her for months. Can he look her in the eye? Can he share more with her than his body? Can he truly be intimate with her (we must remind ourselves that sex and intimacy are not the same)? Can he share his innermost thoughts with her, or listen attentively when she divulges her heart? The answer is clearly no. The guilt eats him from the inside out and consumes any ability to be present, engaged, and loving. While he can go through the external, bodily motions, he cannot share himself. The same is true of God. While forgiving our sins is wonderful, there is still the subjective experience of guilt. Whatever is meant by "guilt" in Psalm 32:5 specifically, we must emphasize that God not only forgives the sin but also comes to take away the subjective guilt that will otherwise plague the heart and suffocate faith, hope, and love. God truly desires us as friends—friends who know his voice, sing his songs, and find great pleasure and deep joy in doing his work.

God desires that his children live with hearts unburdened by the weight of sin's guilt. So how do we receive God's forgiveness and be freed from the subjective guilt that threatens to suffocate our hearts and snuff out any chance for faith, hope, and love? David shows us the way in Psalm 32:5. We simply need to be honest with God. That's all. There's no long or complicated formula—just a child being honest with their Daddy. Longman writes: "forgiveness does not come automatically, but only after confession and repentance."[7] God does the heavy lifting but something is still required of us.

Truth is the soil where freedom blooms. From the moment Adam and Eve covered themselves with fig leaves and shrank into the shadows of the garden, humanity has been perfecting the art of concealment—*what dark artists we have become!* Unfortunately, we are masters at hiding which is to our present and eternal detriment. We must choose to go against the grain of our fallen human nature and not hide from God. Psalm 62:8 offers this encouragement: "Trust in him at all times, you people; pour out your hearts to him, for God is our refuge." This includes confessing our sins! When we pour out our hearts to God in confession, daring to trust in his extravagant mercy, we open the door to the cleansing waters of his forgiveness—waters that not only remove the sin but also wash away the subjective guilt.

He heals us.

He restores us.

The friendship can grow again.

There is also a strong connection between receiving God's forgiveness and being there for others. While Paul instructs us in Galatians 6:2 to carry each other's burdens,

---

7. Longman III, *Psalms: An Introduction and Commentary*, 165.

only a heart that has been *unburdened* of guilt is truly free to bear the burdens of others, including God's. Only then can we pray prayers like the one that Bob Pierce, founder of World Vision, prayed in the 1940s: "Let my heart be broken by the things that break the heart of God." While focusing on forgiveness and guilt might at times seem overly individualistic, nothing could be further from the truth. It is deeply connected to how we love and serve those God has placed in our lives. A freed heart can truly love because it is no longer preoccupied with itself.

God truly cares for us. He doesn't just want to forgive our sin; he wants to remove the subjective guilt that hinders friendship and destroys intimacy. This guilt has the power to psychologically disable us, leaving us hopeless, ashamed, and ineffective in carrying out God's Kingdom work on earth. For this reason, God desires to address it alongside the sin. This is good news for anyone who longs to both enjoy and share with others the "righteousness, peace, and joy in the Holy Spirit."[8] Therefore, we must continually—even daily—take the step that David took when he prayed, "I acknowledged my sin..." and "I will confess..."

---

8. Rom 14:17

Prayer

Therefore let all the faithful pray to you while you may be found; surely the rising of the mighty waters will not reach them.

~Psalm 32:6

There is a rhythm to Psalm 32, a movement between teaching, testimony, and prayer. In some cases, these are occurring simultaneously. The verse we explored in the last chapter concludes with—"And you forgave the guilt of my sin"—and it marks a high point when David's silence gives way to surrender. It would be easy to assume that David would now return to a teaching mode in verse 6, shifting back into a more instructive posture similar to the first two verses in the psalm. Initially, I thought this was the case. But a closer look reveals something else: *David is still praying*. The line "let all the faithful pray to you" makes this clear. He hasn't stepped away from communion with God; rather, he is still speaking to him—even as he pleads with others to seek the Lord while he may be found. His words remain vertical. The turn away from direct prayer doesn't come until verse 8. Until then, David continues pouring out his heart before the God who met him in his brokenness.

DAVID PRAYS

This highlights an important and somewhat unique feature of Psalm 32: *David frequently shifts voices.* In verses 1–2, we hear his own reflective voice. But in verses 3–7, he is praying—speaking directly to the God who has shown him mercy, forgiven his horrific sins, and lifted the burden of deep-seated guilt. David is both humbled and overjoyed, and what begins to spill out is the gratitude of a heart set free. As we will see, God himself then speaks in verses 8–9[1], followed by David's voice to conclude the psalm in verses 10–11.

David's heart is full and has been "stirred by a noble theme."[2] Verse 6 could have read: "Therefore, let all the faithful pray while *he* may be found." Such a phrasing would place David in teaching mode, instructing believers to follow his example in acknowledging sin and receiving God's forgiveness. Yet, this is not what David writes. Instead, he says: "Therefore, let all the faithful pray *to you* while *you* may be found."[3] David is addressing God on behalf of others, not pleading with others on behalf of God. While not the focus of the psalm, these words serve as an implicit reminder that it is wise and efficacious to first talk to God on behalf of others before talking with others about God. Besides, only in close communion with the Lord are we of much *eternal* use to others.

David clearly has someone in mind when he prays, "let all the faithful pray. . ."—he is thinking of God's people. Toward the end of the psalm, David calls all the "righteous" to rejoice, be glad, and sing in view of God's forgiving nature

---

1. Bible scholars disagree on this point, yet writing a book of this nature forces one to assume a position to some degree. This will be discussed in more detail later in the book.

2. Ps 45:1

3. Italics mine

and deeds. Similarly, in verse 6, David cries out to God from a place of peace, joy, and relief, longing for God's entire community to know him in the personal, passionate, and merciful way David now knows. David is back with God, and his heart is overflowing. He now wants the same for others.

He begins verse 6 with the word "therefore," a word that is always significant because it serves as a linguistic bridge, connecting what precedes it with what is about to follow. In verse 5, David has just finished recounting the moment of his breaking: "And you forgave the guilt of my sin." In this declaration, David reflects on one specific aspect of the Lord's beauty: *his forgiving nature.* God is truly the God who forgives, and any soul that has forgotten this unfathomable truth is a soul suffering needlessly. As one commentary puts it, "[David's] experience of answered prayer moves him to pray that all God's people would prove their Lord in the same way."[4] This forgiveness—this indescribably sweet forgiveness that has the power to turn someone's life upside down—must be shared. Others must experience it for themselves. Thus, David cries out to God in prayer, asking him to take action and swiftly work in the lives of other believers to make this same reality known.

MIGHTY WATERS

We now turn to the latter half of verse 6, a phrase that has always been somewhat challenging for me to interpret: "Surely the rising of the mighty waters will not reach them." What does David mean by "mighty waters"? We must be careful not to overthink. Even before consulting sources, one thing is clear: the mighty waters are not intrinsically desirable in this context. The basic idea is that whatever they represent,

---

4. MacDonald, *Believer's Bible Commentary*, 594.

David emphasizes that it is good for them not to reach the believer. It is good to escape them. Even as they rise, the believer has the assurance that they need not drown.

That said, it is best to interpret these words in view of this particular psalm—*it's immediate context*. Peter Craigie writes:

> The godly are invited to pray at "a time of stress" (v 6); the precise nuance of these words is probably to be understood in terms of vv 3–4. Whenever the stress of unrepented sin is experienced, that person must turn to God in a prayer of repentance. The metaphor of the "flood of mighty waters" may imply a torrential flood following rain, whose waters would not reach the person who had prayed in confession to God.[5]

Along these lines, the New Living Translation (NLT) offers helpful insight: "Therefore, let all the godly pray to you while there is still time, that they may not drown in the floodwaters of judgment." The strength of this translation is that it interprets the NIV's "mighty waters" in a way that more clearly aligns with the focus of this psalm. The Contemporary English Version (CEV) is similar to the NLT: "We worship you, Lord, and we should always pray whenever we find out that we have sinned. Then we won't be swept away by a raging flood."

While the language in the NIV and other translations may seem ambiguous at first, it becomes clearer when interpreted in light of this particular psalm. This is why I find the NLT and CEV especially helpful. One Bible commentary notes, "Those who live in fellowship with the Lord will be delivered in a time of distress. The rush of great waters will never reach them." And what is more distressing than a plagued, guilt-ridden conscience? I know of none. While I

---

5. Craigie, *Psalms 1–50*, 267.

made a sincere decision to trust in the person and work of Jesus Christ at age eight, it wasn't until I was 27 that I truly believed God loved me, had grace for me—not just everyone else—and delighted in having me for a son. While my battle with OCD which began at age five surely complicated things, it doesn't change the fact that I spent 19 years of my Christian life miserable. I constantly felt guilty, anxious, and performative with God. It wasn't much of a relationship, even though I was trying so hard and wanted to know him above all else.

But God took charge of my life and led me to a book titled *Grace Works* by Dudley Hall. It literally changed my life, as I explain in greater detail in my book *Heal Me or Kill Me*. This journey is likely one of the reasons why, along with Psalms, Romans is my favorite book in the Bible. It's also why one of my favorite authors is the late Brennan Manning. He understood what it meant to feel like a loser and still drink deeply of the love and mercy of God.

Maybe David is encouraging all of us—both then and now—not to allow the guilt, anxiety, depression, and hopelessness that often result from unconfessed sin to keep rising in our hearts. Matthew Henry writes: "But the true and only way to peace of conscience, is, to confess our sins, that they may be forgiven; to declare them that we may be justified."[6] We must run to God and pray to him while he may be found. If we do, we will not be overcome by the dark, tumultuous waters that threaten.

If you have trusted in Jesus Christ, he has forgiven you, and this divine act of mercy has cleared the way for you and the Father to walk together throughout life. To find the Lord is to be in his presence and live keenly aware of his closeness. However, refusing to confess our sin and receive his forgiveness hides and hardens our hearts, preventing us from

---

6. Henry, *Concise Commentary*, Ps 32:3.

recognizing the Lord's kind and helpful presence. Thus, it is only through confessing our sin and receiving his forgiveness that we can once again realize the nearness of the Lord and keep the waters at bay.

I've always found it both paradoxical and tragic that the Lord can be near to someone, even while that person remains distant from him. It is a mystery, no doubt. Only when we become fully aware of his presence can we stand securely, as though perched on a rock, beyond the reach of the mighty waters. It brings to mind the final scene in The Lord of the Rings films, where Frodo and Sam lie together on a rock, surrounded by fire and ruin after the destruction of Mount Doom. They have no strength left and nowhere to go, yet for a moment, they rest. It is there, on that rock, that the eagles come and carry them to safety. Sometimes, all we need is a safe, secure place to lie down and rest until God's salvation—in whatever form is needed in that season—comes. As God's children, we can be sure that help is on the way. He has promised it. In the meantime, he wants to teach us what it means for him to be our hiding place, our refuge, our shelter. God's presence is our supreme resting place, and David longs for others to know and experience what he has come to know firsthand. He has escaped the waters, and he wants all of God's people to enjoy the same. As Psalm 103 wonderful celebrates, there are benefits to knowing God!

This sets the stage beautifully for the next verse, where worshipful proclamation and intimate, hope-filled words erupt from David's heart.

Hiding Place

You are my hiding place; you will protect me from trouble and surround me with songs of deliverance.

~Psalm 32:7

When I read verse 7, the word that comes to mind is *safety*. Safety is a concept that permeates the modern mind—for better or worse. We hear it in phrases like: "Is this neighborhood safe?" "I want this to be a safe space," "She didn't feel safe in the relationship," "The team played it too safe," or "This is a safe investment." Depending on the context, safety can be good or bad. Sometimes it points to wisdom and protection and at other times, it reveals fear, avoidance, or a lack of courage.

The Lord desires to be a safe place for those who trust in him. This is the good kind of safety. On the night before his crucifixion, Jesus told His disciples, "I have called you friends."[1] Approximately 1,000 years before John penned these words, Solomon wrote, "There is a friend who sticks closer than a brother."[2] While there are certainly times when God seems more like a lion than a lamb, this does not change the fact that he is most gentle, kind, and gracious toward

1. John 15:15
2. Prov 18:24

those who admit their desperate need for him and long for his presence. Put simply, he is a safe place for his children—those who trust in Christ as their Savior and Lord. He is a very real hiding place where we can be weak, find comfort, unload our burdens in prayer, and "receive mercy and grace to help us in our time of need."[3] We are not alone.

HIDING PLACE

Verse 7 is where David concludes the prayer that began in verse 3. While he is recounting past events, he is doing so while prayerfully speaking directly to God. Few phrases in God's Word are sweeter to repeat than, "You are my hiding place." I picture David pausing for a moment, taking a deep breath, lifting his eyes to the sky, and whispering these intimate words. When you read through this psalm, do not rush past them. These are not fast words, nor can they be appreciated in haste. I encourage you to pause for two or three minutes, close your eyes, and repeat them prayerfully to God, giving the Spirit time to weave them into the fabric of your soul.

> You are my hiding place.
>
> You are my hiding place.
>
> You are my hiding place.

God is *your* hiding place. God is *my* hiding place. God is *our* hiding place. These truly are remarkable words. How is it that the God of the universe—the one who created ex nihilo with "mere" words, who parted the Red Sea and the

---

3. Heb 4:16

Jordan River, who is responsible for the highest mountains and the most glorious waterfalls—is also a hiding place for messy, broken people? The omnipotent Creator and majestic God—the one true God—is also the safest place for us to turn. Only Christ and his cross have made it so.

David's words remind me of a powerful story of refuge and trust: Corrie Ten Boom's *The Hiding Place*. During World War II, Corrie and her family hid Jews in their home, creating a literal "hiding place" to protect them from Nazi persecution. This physical shelter symbolized something far greater—the spiritual refuge found in God alone. Even after their arrest and imprisonment in Ravensbrück concentration camp, Corrie and her sister Betsie clung to this truth. In *The Hiding Place*, Corrie Ten Boom recounts the time when her sister was horribly sick:

> Sleet stung as we reached the outside. I stepped close to the stretcher to form a shield for Betsie. We walked past the waiting line of sick people, through the door, and into a large ward. They placed the stretcher on the floor and I leaned down to make out Betsie's words, "must tell people what we have learned here. We must tell them that there is no pit so deep that He is not deeper still. They will listen to us, Corrie, because we have been here."[4]

While Betsie died shortly before Corrie was released from Ravensbrück in 1944, Corrie would share her sister's profound words for decades to come: "There is no pit so deep, that God's love is not deeper still." This intimate expression of faith reflects the essence of Psalm 32:7, illustrating that God serves as a refuge not only from external threats but also from internal turmoil. Emphasizing the internal is crucial, as we often have no control over external events in our lives. If

---

4. ten Boom, *The Hiding* Place, 285.

God was a real, tangible hiding place for Corrie and Betsie in a place as horrific and inhumane as Ravensbrück, then he can definitely be that for us. We must only allow him. He stands ready and waiting with a gentle shepherd's heart. He truly is the God of all comfort,[5] a Wonderful Counselor,[6] and a Prince of Peace.[7] In the apostle Paul's words: "For I am convinced that neither death nor life, neither angels nor demons, neither the present nor the future, nor any powers, neither height nor depth, nor anything else in all creation, will be able to separate us from the love of God that is in Christ Jesus our Lord."[8]

While God sometimes offers help by changing something in the external world, he often does not. Instead, he offers his comforting, hope-filled, perspective-changing presence. Refusing to remove that which is causing anguish—he has never been interested in quick fixes—he offers himself, as if to say: "My child, I am with you and will help you, even in the midst of that which I will not currently change for you." This can feel harsh unless one possesses a desire, if only a crumb, to know him more. He will be known by those who want to know him.

David chose to make God his hiding place. What stands out most to me in these beautiful words is the contrast found between "You are my hiding place" in verse 7 and the language in verse 3: ". . . your hand was heavy on me; my strength was sapped. . ." Tripp writes: "there's a big contrast in this Psalm between the moment when the writer of the Psalm is silent, refusing to confess, and the beauty of the moment when he confesses his sin."[9] Within only a few sentences, David went

5. 2 Cor 1:3
6. Isa 9:6
7. Isa 9:6
8. Rom 8:38–39
9. Tripp, "Psalm 32."

from describing God as the one who had applied great pressure on his conscience—draining his strength—to the one who had become his hiding place. What changed? Not God. He is the same yesterday, today, and forever.[10] The only thing that changed was David's heart. He went from being prideful, stubborn, unrepentant, and distant from God to broken and humble. He fell on the rock before it crushed him. It was David that changed, not God. This inner shift, this sweet transformation, completely changed David's perspective. God was no longer the one applying pressure; instead, he was David's hiding place—*his safe place*. David was now free to walk and live closely with his God once more.

The simple truth is that repentance—which includes confession of sin but involves much more—opens the heart and removes obstacles (mental, emotional, spiritual), paving the way for God's grace to touch every aspect of our lives once again. In a sense, one must choose between being consumed by the mighty waters or by God—the choice is ours. Repentance is choosing God, making way for reconciliation and healing. He doesn't need us to jump over a thousand hurdles or perform a million good deeds to earn our way back into his good graces. Instead, he simply wants us to humble ourselves, confess our sin, admit our need for him, and tell him we want him back in our lives.

While these actions never earn God's forgiveness, they are necessary to receive it. Henry writes: "Although repentance and confession do not merit the pardon of transgression, they are needful to the real enjoyment of forgiving mercy."[11] This is an important reminder. Although certain steps are required for us to accept and enjoy God's mercy, the steps never earn it; they simply open us to receive it.

---

10. Heb 13:8
11. Henry, *Concise Commentary*, Ps 32:3.

PROTECTION FROM TROUBLE

The second part of the verse presents a challenge. At first glance, it seems to claim something that contradicts our lived experience: "you will protect me from trouble." God obviously does *not* protect us from all trouble, so what does David mean by this? How are we to understand these words in view of our experience? On the surface, one could argue that David's life was characterized by *trouble*—sometimes stemming from God's call and, at other times, from his own failings. God did not shield David from trouble entirely; in fact, his life was an ongoing combination of conflicts, struggles, and crises. He even writes in Psalm 34:19: "The righteous person may have many troubles, but the Lord delivers him from them all."

Who among us could honestly say that God has protected them from all trouble, as these words might initially suggest? Simply put, he has not. Many of us have experienced unwanted events (putting it nicely), been hurt by others, struggled financially, watched dreams crumble, been disappointed by mentors and spiritual leaders, experienced abuse of some sort, lost someone we deeply loved, and suffered in numerous other ways as well. *God obviously doesn't protect us from all trouble, so what does David mean here?*

We are faced with two options. We can either interpret God's Word superficially and ignore what our experience seems to suggest, or we can revisit Scripture and ask, "How should these words be properly understood in light of our experience?" While some evangelicals might cringe at the idea of biblical interpretation and experience being mentioned together, the reality is that experience matters. When building our theology, we should never grant our experience the same authority as that which is revealed in God's Word. On the other hand, neither should we discount our experience entirely. Our experience should never override God's Word when the two clearly contradict each other, but when they don't, we should not hesitate to reevaluate our understanding of Scripture if our experience seems to challenge it.

With that in mind, I begin by affirming two truths—one drawn from Scripture and the other from experience:

1. David prayed and believed that God would protect him from trouble.
2. God does not *always* shield his people from trouble but allows it to enter their lives.

These two truths, though seemingly at odds, invite us into a deeper exploration of how God's promises and our lived realities coexist. 19th-century pastor and theologian Charles Spurgeon offers two possible interpretations:

> That which troubled others never troubled them; or else the phrase must have this sense, that though they be troubled with their troubles, though God submit them so far to the common condition of men, that they be sensible of them, yet he shall preserve them from that trouble so as that it shall never overthrow them, never sink them into a dejection of spirit, or diffidence in his mercy! they shall find storms, but a stout and strong ship under foot.[12]

Spurgeon is trying to make sense of the tension here between what God's inerrant word affirms and what we know by our experience. Neither should be dismissed easily, although only God's Word (i.e., the Bible) possesses *magisterial* authority. On one hand, Spurgeon suggests that the passage could mean that Christians are not troubled by the things that trouble others. While this may be true at times, I don't think it is the best interpretation. After all, we often see Christians troubled

---

12. Spurgeon, *The Treasury of David: Psalms 27–57*, 97.

by some of the same things that trouble unbelievers. We are all human, after all, and no one is shielded from trouble.

Spurgeon then offers a second way to understand this phrase in Psalm 32:7. Perhaps we do face many of the same troubles—"the common condition of men"—but God promises that we will never be utterly overcome or defeated by them. In Spurgeon's words, Christ remains a "stout and strong ship under foot" even in the worst of storms. So, while God allows trouble to come our way, he preserves us in the sense that these troubles will never have the final word. As long as we stay close to the Father and remain open to his helpful graces, we can walk in victory and not be utterly cast down.

I am sympathetic to this second interpretation. Years ago, I read a book by Christian psychologist Dan Allender titled *The Healing Path: How the Hurts in Your Past Can Lead You to a More Abundant Life*. I no longer have the book on hand, but I remember the major premise upon which the entire book was built: *Don't waste your pain*. The message was simple and powerful. The reality is that we all suffer; there is no escaping it. As Christians, we are not exempt. We do not cease to be human when we become a Christian. If we must suffer, we might as well derive something from the pain to carry with us on the journey. It's a practical suggestion, no doubt, yet it's grounded in God's supernatural presence, power, and willingness to work within us and bring beauty from ashes. This is Kingdom alchemy.

Another possible interpretation is that when David referred to trouble, he was thinking specifically of lingering guilt. This would make sense in view of the psalm. We can hide in him from past sin and failure, refusing to let the negative, self-accusing waters drown our hearts and damage our relationship with the Lord. The waters cannot reach us because we are hidden in Christ. When the Father of Lies comes to suggest that what we have done is too bad for God to completely forgive, we run to Christ. We allow the voice of God to drown out the accusing voice of Satan who roams about seeking someone to devour. We hide in Christ by running to the Word, pouring over the truth, and taking shelter in what God has declared about our sin and guilt. When we do, God's truth grows louder than the enemy's voice—*we are transformed by the renewing of our minds.*[13] Truth wins as we hide in Christ and his truth, but we must go to him.

The option to hide in Christ is truly one of the greatest benefits for Christians who have been forgiven, cleansed, and declared righteous in his sight (i.e., justification). Countering one of the main consequences of sin—"I was afraid . . . so I hid"[14]—we instead enter God's presence boldly and sing: "Praise the Lord, my soul, and forget not all his benefits . . . who forgives all your sins . . ."[15] In the end, we either hide *from* God or hide *in* God—a choice that determines everything else about our lives.

SONGS OF DELIVERANCE

The verse concludes with, "surround me with songs of deliverance." Here we are given the wonderful picture of a singing God—a God who delights not only in speech but in song. David has already declared God to be a hiding place, one who protects him from trouble. Now he identifies him as one who, through beautiful song, has the power to deliver from the objective guilt of sin, the subjective flood of guilty feelings, and the potential trouble that might have come had he continued to resist God.

---

13. Rom 12:2
14. Gen 3:10
15. Ps 103:2–3

Psalm 32

One of my favorite scenes in fiction is from C.S. Lewis' *The Magician's Nephew*. In it, Digory, Polly, the Cabby, Uncle Andrew, Queen Jadis, and various creatures watch and listen as Aslan, the great lion, sings Narnia into existence.

> In the darkness something was happening at last. A voice had begun to sing . . . the most beautiful noise he had ever heard. It was so beautiful he could hardly bare it . . . . One moment there had been nothing but darkness; next moment a thousand, thousand points of light leaped out—single stars, constellations, and planets . . . . The Lion was pacing to and fro about that empty land and singing his new song. It was softer and more lifting than the song by which he had called up the stars and the sun; a gentle, rippling music . . . . And when he burst into a rapid series of lighter notes she was not surprised to see primroses suddenly appearing in every direction.[16]

While Aslan could have simply spoken creation into being, he chooses instead to sing, a strictly unnecessary yet wonderful aesthetic touch. He is the singing lion, and here in Psalm 32, we find a singing God. While I cannot say for certain, I imagine Lewis had Aslan sing because some have speculated that God created all that there is through song. In Genesis 1 and 2, God *creates* through song, and in Psalm 32, he is the God who *delivers* through song.

The God of Christianity is a singing, joyful, and powerful God. David is now declaring, worshiping, and celebrating the God with whom relationship has been restored. God is once again his hiding place—kind, powerful, and preserving. And he is the singing God who, with a single melody, can scatter every demon and heal every hurt.

---

16. Lewis, *The Magician's Nephew*, 93, 97, 99.

Guidance

I will instruct you and teach you in the way you should go; I will counsel you with my loving eye on you. Do not be like the horse or the mule, which have no understanding but must be controlled by bit and bridle or they will not come to you.

~Psalm 32:8–9

Psalm 32:8 has always held a special place in my heart. I have cherished its words and longed for their reality with all my heart: *to be intimately guided by the Lord each day.* I remember first being struck by Psalm 32:8 when reading the New King James Version (NKJV): "I will instruct you and teach you in the way you should go; I will guide you with My eye." Anyone with a long-term friend or good marriage knows what this means. A glance of the eye, a tilt of the head, or a certain facial expression can speak volumes—but this kind of communication only happens between those who are close, who have put in the long, hard work that intimacy requires over the years.

However, it never occurred to me that anyone other than God might be speaking these words. In my naivety, I took them at face value, assumed they were God's, and drank deeply. While I still believe that God is speaking these words to David—and by extension, to all his people—I acknowledge that contemporary scholarship tends to favor the view that David is actually the one addressing the faithful here.

A BEAUTIFUL PROMISE

I now know that the NKJV's rendering of the original Hebrew is not the most accurate, and for that reason, I no longer focus on this particular wording. Still, other translations have proven similarly beautiful. As moving as these words are when viewed as coming from God's own mouth, it is only fair to admit that scholars are divided on the speaker's identity in Psalm 32:8–9. Older interpreters, including Luther, understood them as God's direct speech to the forgiven sinner. While some more recent interpreters continue this view, others—like Calvin long ago—believed these are David's words, addressing the community and pointing others to the God who forgave him.[1]

Both interpretations offer rich insight: one emphasizes God as the ultimate teacher, while the other highlights David's role as a guide for others, drawing from his personal journey of repentance and forgiveness. I find it difficult to decide definitively whether Psalm 32:8–9 represents God speaking directly or David addressing the assembly. Though I see the risks of this interpretive approach, I'm drawn to the view that God is speaking in the first person because I want the psalm to read that way. I cherish these words and find them especially beautiful, sweet, and profoundly moving when I imagine then coming directly from God rather than through David. Yet, I cannot ignore how David consistently shifts voices throughout Psalm 32.

---

1. Lange et al., *A Commentary on the Holy Scriptures: Psalms*, 225.

Before spending most of the chapter exploring the perspective of God speaking, I want to briefly give fair consideration to the alternative view. In other words, what if this is David speaking to his readers rather than God speaking to David? David begins by introducing the topic of forgiveness in verses 1-2, then transitions to addressing God in verses 3-7. After recounting his personal experience, it feels fitting that he might pivot to address the assembly, positioning himself as a teacher with a heartfelt plea: "Let me teach you! Let me help you! Come, I will instruct you so that you do not do as I did and delay God's blessings in your life." After all, the psalm includes the word "maskil" in the heading which is often understood to mean a teaching psalm or psalm of instruction. It is not only meant for worship, but to instruct in the ways of God so that people can live more faithfully.

This heartfelt plea for those less mature in the faith to listen, learn, and grow from his experience rather than through the school of hard knocks—a concept psychologist Alfred Bandura termed "observational learning"[2]—is beautifully echoed in the words: "If you do not know, most beautiful of women, follow the tracks of the sheep and graze your young goats by the tents of the shepherds."[3] In other words, do not hesitate to glean from those who have walked this path before, who know the ways and wisdom of God and can spare you much heartache and delay on the pilgrim's journey. Here, David is the sage, the wise one, and he is sharing his experienced-laced wisdom with any and all who will listen.

All of this to say that I see the merit to both positions. *Theologically*, I take a middle path and commit to neither view exclusively; I can see both sides. One commentary explains:

---

2. Observational learning is a process through which individuals acquire new behaviors, skills, or information by watching others rather than through direct experience or instruction.

3. Song 1:8

There is a question as to whether verses 8 and 9 are the words of David or of the Lord. If we interpret them as David's language, then they remind us . . . that "the natural response of forgiveness is to help others by sharing one's own experience and specifically by counseling others in trouble." If we adopt the other view, then it is the Lord replying to David's worship with a promise of guidance and a lesson on the need for constant yieldedness. It is the Father spreading a feast for the returned backslider.[4]

One thing that we can be sure of is that no matter the view one adopts, these words apply to us now, regardless of whether they were originally from God to David or from David to the faithful. Human nature has not changed. People resisted God then, and we—including you and me—resist him now. Whether these words come directly from God or from David, they remain good words—wise, true, and helpful for all disciples of Jesus striving to follow him.

Devotionally, however, I cannot help but embrace the perspective I have always favored: *it is God who is speaking directly to David in verses 8 and 9*. If this is correct, then verse 8 becomes one of the most beautiful, poetic, and hope-filled promises in all of Scripture.

God will instruct us.

God will guide us.

His loving eyes are and will always remain fixed on us.

We are never alone.

---

[4]. MacDonald, *Believer's Bible Commentary*, 594–95.

While most translations closely resemble the NIV's rendering, "I will counsel you with my loving eye on you," I do want to say one more thing about the New King James Version's wording which is particularly striking: "I will guide you with my eye." On this wording, Guzik writes:

> The idea is of one who waits upon another so attentively that a mere look at the eye indicates the will. A butler waiting upon his master at dinner can illustrate this; the master need only look at the salt shaker and the butler understands that he wants it.[5]

This language is intimate and seems more akin to what God might say to David than what David might say to fellow pilgrims. *This is the main reason I believe that God is speaking here rather than David.* Of course, I could be wrong, but I do not read the words, "I will guide you with my eye" or "my loving eye on you" and immediately think: "Oh, this must be David writing to his fellow Israelites." Instead, it strikes me as God's voice, the voice of the ultimate Lover, the voice of the one who would later designate the church as his bride, the voice of the one that would rather feel nails pierce his flesh than go without a people. While respecting the different views of scholars, one would be hard pressed to convince me otherwise: *the language is too sweet, too intimate, too close.* God is speaking, the ultimate Shepherd and Husband, promising to do what he has always desired: *guide us.* In David's words: "He guides me along the right paths for his name's sake."[6] He longs to do this in our lives today, this very minute. Our proper response is to cherish this promise and invite the Lord prayerfully: "Show me your ways, Lord, teach me your paths. Guide me in your truth and teach me, for you are God my Savior, and my hope is in you all day long."[7] The Holy Spirit awaits.

5. Guzik, "Study Guide for Psalm 32."
6. Ps 23:3
7. Ps 25:4–5

PSALM 32

How can something so profoundly good be so undeniably true? If these words are indeed from God to every believer, can a sweeter promise—apart from that of forgiveness—be found anywhere in Scripture? The prophet Isaiah writes: "Whether you turn to the right or to the left, your ears will hear a voice behind you, saying, 'This is the way; walk in it.'"[8] God is always present with his kids, and like any good father or mother, he delights in talking to us and sharing his wisdom.

PROFOUNDLY LOGICAL

Now consider the placement of verse 8—it doesn't open the psalm. It only appears *after* David has confessed and repented of his sins and received God's forgiveness. The positioning of verse 8 is *profoundly logical*. When the heart is hard and closed off to God—when it is desensitized to his promptings—how can it be led? A foot leaves a mark in sand, not rock; a thumbprint is impressed upon soft material, not stone. When we choose to sin and then refuse to confess it, the weight of guilt drains us, suffocates us, and hardens our hearts. As one author writes, "Some burdens are so heavy that they seem to consume all our strength. No burden is heavier than the burden of guilt."[9] Our spiritual antennas wither and fade, leaving us deaf to God's voice—his nudging, promptings, and whispers. In that state, we are dead inside, like a walking pile of bricks—heavy, inflexible, unmoldable, and unresponsive.

When the soul breaks and forgiveness comes, God not only removes the sin but also the guilt we feel. The disciple enjoys the sweetness of a clean conscience. How wonderful

---

8. Isa 30:21
9. Ellsworth, *Opening up Psalms, Opening Up Commentary*, 95.

it is to live with a light heart, free of guilt. What could be better? The soul is set free to float and fly again. Even more, it is now ready to be led. That's the point.

The logical flow of the psalm is overwhelmingly simple and clear: *a person repents, is forgiven, their conscience is cleansed, and their heart made pliable to the Spirit's promptings.* Forgiveness clears, cleans, and softens the heart, leaving us broken, humble, and receptive. In this state, God can work freely; the person is soft, surrendered, and sensitive to his leadership. Forgiveness always paves the way for greater intimacy and better communication.

How many hearts in the church today are truly sensitive to the Spirit's voice? Am I? Are you? We love our Bibles—but what about the Spirit? I recently shared in a sermon that until age 13, I grew up in a denomination that made me think of the Trinity as the Father, Son, and the other guy. The last of the three was unknowable, more of a power or force that helps us in some ambiguous way with loving the other two. But this is not a biblical view. The Holy Spirit is a person, and when we are enjoying peace with God, God the Holy Spirit—the third person of the Trinity—can guide us easily. How many genuinely believe in, and earnestly desire, the Spirit's constant leading, prompting, guiding, and nudging? It's an honest question, because deep down, we often want our own way. And yet, God knocks at the door, ready to instruct, teach, and guide. When forgiveness comes and softens the heart, Jesus' promise can be realized: "My sheep hear my voice."

Forgiven.

Cleansed.

Softened.

Psalm 32

Surrendered.

Open.

Sensitive.

Available.

The space between God's voice and our soul is now unobstructed. All is clear. You and I can live tethered to his voice, taking delight in every whisper and word. How foolish it is to be offered the divine voice throughout life, yet rely solely on reason, pro and con lists, and our fallible intuition! One of the greatest gifts God can give is to make a human being desperate to hear, follow, and build their life around the sound and wisdom of his voice. That desperation demands our attention.

Being able to hear this voice opens the door for God to do wonderful things in us and through us. Psalm 29—which is essentially a meditation on the beauty and power of God's voice—says that the voice of the Lord is "powerful" and "majestic," able to "break the cedars [of Lebanon]," "strike with flashes of lightning," "shake the desert," "make the deer give birth," and "strip the forests bare."[10] To live without hearing God's voice is to forfeit so much of what Christ purchased for every believer through his death on the cross and his resurrection. The voice of the Lord can now fill the earth—including our hearts and every sphere of our lives—no longer wasted on a hardened heart. We can pray with John: "The bride belongs to the bridegroom. The friend who attends the bridegroom waits and listens for him, and is full of joy when

---

10. Ps 29:4–5, 7–9

he hears the bridegroom's voice. That joy is mine, and it is now complete."[11]

HORSES AND MULES

Verse 9 can be seen as a kind of footnote to verse 8. After promising to instruct, teach, and guide with his counsel, God offers a vivid contrast: *the image of a stubborn horse or mule that must be controlled with bit and bridle to be made obedient.* The options boil down to two: being guided by the Lord in love or trusting in our own ability to guide ourselves. As human beings, we can sugarcoat this all we want and use sophisticated terminology to suggest there are other existential options, but in the end, every person chooses to trust either the Lord or themselves. C.S. Lewis poignantly writes, "There are only two kinds of people in the end: those who say to God, 'Thy will be done,' and those to whom God says, in the end, 'Thy will be done.' All that are in Hell, choose it."[12] While Lewis's quote focuses more broadly on salvation, it speaks to the spirit of Psalm 32, where the believer experiences the consequences of resisting God but is also offered the gift of divine guidance—if they will receive it. God will not force us. Even in the face of Christ's atoning death—he is the only way, the truth, and the life[13]—God grants us the freedom to either embrace or reject him. Why else would he have created the Tree of the Knowledge of Good and Evil? This freedom underscores one of the most sobering realities of the human condition: *that God, in his desire for genuine love, permits us to make the worst choice imaginable—the choice to live without him.*

---

11. John 3:29
12. Lewis, *The Great Divorce*, 75.
13. John 14:6

There is one more interesting point about verse 9. It ends with the words: "or they will not come to you." I would have expected something different—something focused more on behavior, obedience, or duty. But that's not what we find, and I'm glad for it. The emphasis is relational: "not come to you." When we read verses 3–5, we feel the emotional and spiritual distance that resulted from David's refusal to repent. But after he repents, he immediately writes, "let all the faithful pray to you. . ." In other words, let all who repent do what he has done: *return to the Lord*. Let them come. *Let us come*. The relationship has been repaired; reconciliation has taken place.

Ultimately, two visions of the Christian life are presented: those who believe and are surrendered to the Lord, and those who, while believing, still resist him—like David once did. This second group resembles the believers Paul described when he wrote: "Brothers and sisters, I could not address you as people who live by the Spirit but as people who are still worldly—mere infants in Christ. I gave you milk, not solid food, for you were not yet ready for it. Indeed, you are still not ready. You are still worldly."[14] Instead of being stubborn, we can draw near to the Lord with a simple, undivided heart, totally surrendered to his guidance in light of what he has done for us. Being forgiven, our conscience can be clean and light so that we are easily led by the Spirit from one situation to the next.

---

14. 1 Cor 3:1–3.

Love

Many are the woes of the wicked, but the Lord's unfailing love surrounds the one who trusts in him.
~Ps 32:10

CAN WE IMAGINE ANYTHING better than being surrounded with the Lord's unfailing love?

>Surrounded.

>Immersed.

>Drenched.

>Covered.

>Shielded.

>Insulated.

>Delighted.

Psalm 32

Somehow, in a way that autonomous reason cannot grasp, the Creator and Majestic Lord of all, wants to surround each one of us with his "never stopping, never giving up, unbreaking, always and forever love."[1] It is the same love that Jesus said would characterize his church and serve as the greatest apologetic of both his existence and goodness: "By this everyone will know that you are my disciples, if you love one another."[2] It is a love that surrounds, takes root, permeates, consumes, and then flows out. It is a love that is meant to be both enjoyed and shared. It is for the rich and poor, the intelligent and unintelligent, the young and old, the happy and sad, the lost and found, the accomplished and the unaccomplished. It is a love for all of us—what we desperately need if we are to avoid flaky, insecure identities that rise and fall with our thoughts, feelings, and actions from one day to the next.

Nothing is better than his love.

You need it.

I need it.

Every local church needs it.

Every atheist, agnostic, Christian, and theologian needs it.

In this beautiful verse towards the end of Psalm 32, God makes it clear that he wants to envelop us in this love.

---

1. Lloyd-Jones, *The Jesus Storybook Bible*, 36.
2. John 13:35

WOES OF THE WICKED

While the shining aspect of this verse is the mention of the God's unfailing love, it interestingly begins with a mention of the many woes of the wicked. Why? Even more interesting, do these words imply that the righteous—those that are in Christ by grace and through faith—will not have many troubles?

I cannot read the opening words of Psalm 32:10 without immediately thinking of Psalm 34:19: "The righteous person may have many troubles. . ." This tension reminds us that interpreting Scripture requires careful hermeneutics—the practice of understanding texts in light of their broader context. *Scripture interprets Scripture.* Without this discipline, we risk isolating a word, phrase, or sentence, twisting it to mean whatever we desire. This is the difference between imposing our own meaning on the text (eisegesis)—a postmodern approach stemming from the anti-authoritarian view that meaning does not inhere in the text— and uncovering the meaning already present within it (exegesis). The interplay between Psalm 32:10, Psalm 34:19, and other passages invites us to engage with Scripture carefully, avoiding simplistic conclusions that may reflect more of our fallen human nature than God's truth.

When reading Psalm 32:10, it is crucial to consider what the Bible teaches elsewhere. Whether reflecting on Psalm 34:19, the trials David and Joseph faced on their paths to fulfill their callings, the challenges that confronted Esther, the hurtful whispers and rejection that Joseph and Mary must have endured from family and friends that did not understand, the suffering and martyrdom of many disciples, or even the ultimate example of Jesus on the cross, it becomes clear that this verse cannot mean God's people will be exempt from trouble ("woes") simply because they belong to him. The opposite sometimes seems true. Church history is filled with accounts of those who loved God deeply and endured immense hardship for the sake of his name and kingdom. In the words of a well-known hymn: "This world is not my home, I'm just a passing through."[3]

To be a Christian is to suffer. Troubles come. Years ago, I was struck by a simple truth when reading John 16: there is no season in life, no matter how difficult, that is without joy. And there is also no season in life, no matter how wonderful, that is without pain. Every season—although in unequal proportions—contains both joy and pain. Yet no matter what we face, and no matter what season we are in, there is hope. Paul himself writes to the Christians in Rome:

> Who shall separate us from the love of Christ? Shall trouble or hardship or persecution or famine or nakedness or danger or sword? As it is written: "For your sake we face death all day long; we are considered as sheep to be slaughtered." No, in all these things we are more than conquerors through him who loved us.[4]

While Paul probably didn't have Psalm 32:10 on his mind when he wrote this, he is referring to the Lord's *unfailing love* that surrounds us and helps us overcome. If we are honest, we would prefer God simply get rid of the trouble rather than walk us through it. But God doesn't in most cases—"We can't go over it. We can't go under it. Oh, no! We've got to go through it!"[5] Through God's personal, powerful, and comforting love, we can make it through. His love surrounds us; it will never leave us.

The complete and full testimony of Scripture is unmistakable: *God's people will face trouble after trouble.*

---

3. Brumley, "This World Is Not My Home," 1919.
4. Rom 8:35–37
5. Rosen, *We're Going on a Bear Hunt.*

Mysteriously, some are *called* to face more pain than others. Any message suggesting otherwise is a deceptive lie, offering promises of great pleasure with little pain—a dangerous delusion that sets people up for tremendous disappointment in the Christian life.

Such false expectations often lead to disillusionment and, ultimately, a departure from the Lord when hardship inevitably comes. Christians in the affluent West—and around the world—must be mentally fortified with God's truth so that our "house" does not fall when the rains come, the streams rise, and the winds blow and beat against us. Having realistic expectations grounded in God's Word is like building our house on the rock instead of sand—it is vital.[6] We must "be transformed by the renewing of [our] mind"[7] so that we are not "blown and tossed by the wind"[8] by all-consuming doubts that result from not knowing God's truth.

I can't help but think Psalm 32:10 might read better if it began: "Many are the woes of the wicked and the Christian..." This phrasing would more accurately capture the full biblical witness. Yet, David is making a particular point here, and if anyone understood that loving God doesn't exempt a person from trouble, it was David. Granted, David sometimes brought trouble upon himself through his sin, but there were also times when trouble came through no fault of his own. This is a reality we all experience. So, what can we take from this verse? What is David communicating to us within the broader context of Psalm 32?

To be clear, I do believe that loving God and walking closely with Jesus protects Christians from certain troubles. Following Jesus often spares us from the destructive consequences of sinful behavior, such as the relational and

6. Matt 7:24–27
7. Rom 12:2
8. James 1:6

emotional pain caused by dishonesty, addiction, or infidelity.[9] Walking with God provides wisdom and discernment, helping us avoid unnecessary troubles that arise from poor choices. As Psalm 119:105 says, "Your word is a lamp for my feet, a light on my path." What is the purpose of this light if not to guide us in truth, keep us close to Jesus, and help us avoid detours that lead to disobedience? Such detours often bring a mix of unwanted emotions—depression, confusion, anxiety, fear, and even hopelessness—especially when, as Psalm 32:3 reminds us, we remain silent about our sins for any length of time. Psalm 1 also comes to mind.

> Blessed is the one who does not walk in step with the wicked or stand in the way that sinners take or sit in the company of mockers, but whose delight is in the law of the Lord, and who meditates on his law day and night. That person is like a tree planted by streams of water, which yields its fruit in season and whose leaf does not wither—whatever they do prospers. Not so the wicked! They are like chaff that the wind blows away.[10]

Truthfully, walking with God often spares us from many troubles—a reality we should gratefully confess, celebrate, sing about, and preach. Yet even as we rejoice in this truth, we must also acknowledge that trouble still finds its way into our lives. In fact, there are times when trouble comes precisely because we are walking with God.

---

9. This is not to say that all addiction is sin or the product of sin. A much more nuanced discussion would be required to properly address this subject, a topic that would take us too far from our main focus in this book.

10. Ps 1:1–4

UNFAILING LOVE

This is where the last part of Psalm 32:10 shines: "but the Lord's unfailing love surrounds the one who trusts in him." While David notes that the woes of the wicked will be many, he doesn't explicitly state that the righteous will experience fewer woes. So, what is he saying? I believe David is highlighting a profound truth: *though the wicked face many woes, they must endure them without the Lord by their side—and that is the true tragedy.* We all face trouble, and at times, Christians will face hardship specifically because of their faith. Did Jesus not teach, "Blessed are you when people insult you, persecute you and falsely say all kinds of evil against you because of me."[11] The real difference is not whether we encounter trouble but who is with us in the midst of it. Daniel was not alone in the lion's den, and Shadrach, Meshach, and Abednego were not alone in the fiery furnace. Christians have God—the Creator of the universe and Redeemer of humanity—as a father[12] and friend[13]. His presence is the song sung across the pages of Scripture. We are not alone. When trouble comes and the world feels cold, lifeless, and void of hope, God is near. He is present. He is for us, regardless of how loudly our emotions may scream, "darkness is my closest friend."[14]

Yet, there are Christians who are not fully aware of this unfailing love in their daily experience. I once read—though I don't recall the Christian author—that the greatest distance in the universe between two points is the gap between the mind and the heart. The point was simple: *there are different ways of knowing.* You can know a fact with the mind without

11. Matt 5:11
12. Matt 6:9
13. John 15:14–15
14. Ps 88:18

knowing it in a way that impacts the heart and transforms life. I can know in my mind that God is loving, yet live each moment feeling like I am one great disappointment to him—that he is constantly frustrated with me. Truths can be intellectually grasped yet remain a thousand miles away from the heart. This perfectly describes the Pharisees in Jesus' day. Jesus once said of them: "These people honor me with their lips, but their hearts are far from me."[15] This is especially tragic when it comes to God's insane love for each one of us. It is a truth that we cannot stand to live without. When we do, every single area of our life suffers. Everything in the Christian life hinges on that love, and to live without really knowing it is an existential tragedy and waste of the cross. He has declared his love for you, end of discussion.

It is settled.

Receive it.

Believe it.

Build your life on it.

And share it.

I remember a very special day in my life. For the past 20 years, I've made it a habit to wake up early on my birthday to ensure a quiet, unrushed time with the Lord. For some time now, I've had an extra measure of faith on those mornings, believing that God might want to speak something personal to my heart. So I prioritize giving him the space to do so.

---

15. Matt 15:8–9

Sometimes he does, sometimes he doesn't. But I've grown to expect that he just might.

To this day, my 33rd birthday stands out above the rest. I was sitting in my leather chair, with a small table beside me and a window to my left. After just a few minutes, I had an overwhelming sense that the Lord was saying, "I love you, my son." While those are familiar words that we often hear and reflect on, I knew it was the Lord because I felt myself growing emotional as those words lingered. After a few moments, I responded, "Okay, Lord, thank you for these words. But I would like to know—why do you love me?" What he said next is something I've only shared with my wife—*eight words*. It was deeply personal. As soon as I heard them, I began to weep (not just a tear or two). The Lord had zeroed in on me that morning, on my birthday, and spoke something I'm still writing about to this day.

It was a moment I will carry to my grave. The Lord made it clear that he absolutely, unfathomably loves me—and delights in me. I bring him joy as a son. And he wanted my Type A, overperforming, action-oriented heart—the one that struggles to simply be and receive—to know this. He truly is a God of love, and he seeks out special moments to mark our souls with it.

While God's love surrounds all Christians—his Spirit dwells in their hearts, and he is always present with each of his children—this does not mean every child of God is aware of his loving presence. It is possible for God to be near us, surrounding us with his unfailing love, and yet for us to feel as though he is always frustrated or even angry with us. Put simply, we can believe something that isn't true. Thus, while God may be close to us during trouble, surrounding us with his love, we might remain completely unaware of it and for this reason miss out on the peace, joy, and help that his love provides. *One can starve to death with a feast in front them.*

Psalm 32

Something being true is one thing; *eating* and *drinking* the truth another.

While God's love continually surrounds those who trust in him for salvation, it is often only those who actively trust him in their daily lives who become truly aware of it—reaping the emotional and spiritual benefits that such awareness brings. Psalm 32:10 does not simply read that God's unfailing love surrounds us. It teaches that God's unfailing love surrounds the one who *trusts* in him. There is always something required of us—if for nothing else, simply to receive what God desires to give. The apostle Paul reminds Christians everywhere to "work out your own salvation," even as "it is God who works in you to will and to act in order to fulfill his good purpose."[16]

Trusting God for salvation is one thing; trusting him day by day is another. The latter is what opens and sensitizes the heart to recognize and experience his unfailing love, which surrounds us whether we perceive it or not. God's desire is that we take in his love with every breath, think about it early and late, and allow it to take root in every corner and pocket of our lives. Only then can we be at rest, no matter how fast we are moving or how busy we become.

Both Christians and non-Christians endure hardship and face troubles in this life. Yet David reminds us that Christians face such things surrounded by God's intimate and loving presence—and that makes all the difference.

---

16. Phil 2:13

Rejoice

Rejoice in the Lord and be glad, you righteous; sing, all you who are upright in heart!

~Ps. 32:11

This beautiful psalm concludes with what serves as both a command an an invitation.

Rejoice.

Be glad.

Sing!

These are the words David uses to conclude his meditation on and celebration of God's forgiveness and willingness to guide us once again. Like us, David made many mistakes throughout his life. Yet—even if delayed at times, as we see in this psalm—he refused to let sin define him.

Sin never had the final word.

Though he often suffered the consequences of his failures, he always returned to God. He was truly a man after God's own heart.[1] David knew how to mess up, but he also knew how to throw himself at God's feet and receive mercy.

As I mentioned earlier in the book, my dad wrote in his Bible at the end of Psalm 32: "Joy comes from being right with God." This simple statement captures the essence of the psalm. God does not forgive merely for the sake of forgiving; forgiveness is a means to a greater end. What is that end, or goal? It goes by many names, and any of them will do: reconciliation, friendship, or *koinonia* (transliteration from the Greek). Paul writes, "God is faithful, who has called you into fellowship with his Son, Jesus Christ our Lord." The word translated "fellowship" comes from the Greek *koinōnia*, a rich term used throughout the New Testament to denote deep relationship and mutual partnership—whether with God or with others. Ultimately, God forgives so that he might walk with us once again as in Eden, in a close and loving relationship where we know his heart and join him in making that love known. This friendship and partnership with God are what produces the only true joy the human heart can ever know.

God is not opposed to our joy; instead, he is bent on preventing us from wasting a lifetime of pursuing superficial joy *outside* of him. C.S. Lewis writes:

> Indeed, if we consider the unblushing promises of reward and the staggering nature of the rewards promised in the Gospels, it would seem that our Lord finds our desires, not too strong, but too weak. We are half-hearted creatures, fooling about with drink and sex and ambition when infinite joy is offered us, like an ignorant child who wants to go on making mud pies in a slum because he cannot

---

1. Acts 13:22

imagine what is meant by the offer of a holiday at the sea. We are far too easily pleased.[2]

Joy comes from being right with God, and David now invites God's people to join him in finding their greatest joy in him. As David wrote in Psalm 16:11: "You make known to me the path of life; you will fill me with joy in your presence, with eternal pleasures at your right hand." What if Christians were known for their joy? Pause and consider this question. When was the last time you heard a non-Christian describe either Christianity or a Christian using joy-filled language? Sharing the Gospel might be far easier if joy visibly marked our lives.

After all, who isn't drawn to joy?

Who doesn't long to discover its true source?

C. S. Lewis titled his autobiography *Surprised by Joy*—ironically, the name of the woman he would later marry.[3] The experience and promise of joy were frequent themes in his writing and thought. In *Letters to Malcolm: Chiefly on Prayer*, Lewis ends letter seventeen with the striking line: "Joy is the serious business of Heaven."[4] Joy is a fruit of the Spirit[5] and a reality that Christians—the "righteous" and "upright" in Christ—can rightfully claim, receive, and enjoy.

Augustine, one of the greatest minds in the history of the Church and a towering figure in Christian theology,

---

2. Lewis, *The Weight of Glory*, 22.
3. Her full name was Helen Joy Davidman. She was an American poet, writer, and former atheist who converted to Christianity. Lewis and Joy initially developed a close friendship through correspondence, which eventually led to marriage. They were married in a civil ceremony in 1956 and later had a Christian marriage in 1957 when Joy was seriously ill with cancer.
4. Lewis, *Letters to Malcolm*, 93.
5. Gal 5:22–23

writes in the opening lines of *Confessions*: "You arouse him to take joy in praising you . . ."[6] Joy truly is the serious business of Heaven. Yet, joy cannot take root, grow, and flourish in soil that is too hard with pride.[7]

We cannot remain silent.

We cannot hide.

We cannot pretend.

We cannot remain closed.

We must examine ourselves to see if we are resisting God in any pocket or corner of our lives. This is the only pathway to joy. Shortcuts are not allowed.

Socrates once said that the "unexamined life is not worth living." For Socrates, this was both an invitation and a challenge for others to examine themselves, for he believed it was "the greatest good for a man to discuss virtue every day . . ."[8] While unaided introspection and self-examination have their place, Christianity acknowledges that this humanistic method that relies on autonomous, unguided reason is ultimately insufficient. We are not enough for ourselves; our vision is blurry. This is, in part, what theologians mean by "the noetic effects of sin"—the way sin clouds our thinking, distorts our self-perception, and limits our ability to see truth clearly on our own.

---

6. Augustine, *The Confessions*, 1.

7. In the Parable of the Four Soils (Mark 4:1–20; Matt 13:1–23; Luke 8:4–15), Jesus compares the condition of the human heart to different types of soil, showing how its receptiveness to God's Word determines whether it takes root and flourishes or is hindered.

8. Plato, *Apology*, 41.

In contrast, David writes, "Search me, God, and know my heart; test me and know my anxious thoughts. See if there is any offensive way in me, and lead me in the way everlasting."[9] David's approach to self-examination places God at the center—not our rational or intuitive powers. Yes, we must examine ourselves, but only as we allow the Holy Spirit to take the lead. It is a dance. We are never meant to examine ourselves alone. When we do, we risk opening the door to sadness, discouragement, disappointment, or even hopelessness, depending on what we uncover. Truth may come—but without grace. Or a false grace may appear—without truth. As Proverbs 3:3 and John 1:17 remind us, there is no real grace without truth, and no real truth without grace. Biblical grace and truth always go hand in hand—two sides of the same coin.

In these final words, David invites everyone to join him in singing to the Lord. While it's easy to gloss over, there is something profoundly beautiful about this invitation. Back in verse 7, it was God who surrounded David with songs of deliverance. In verse 10, David speaks of being surrounded with Gods' love. Now that God's song had filled and encompassed David's heart, he calls God's people to return that song. It is because God sings over and around us that we are able to sing back to him. His song permeates our hearts and becomes the very song we sing back to him—*his song becomes our song*. Does it not always begin with God and his initiative? He always takes the first step.

Lasting joy belongs only to those who live with a clean conscience in the presence of the Lord. He is with us, and we are with him. Come what may, the forgiven person can live as God's friend once again, with the sound of his voice ever near. Joy fills our lives when our hearts are free from

---

9. Ps 139:23–24

the crushing weight of guilt (subjective), the need to pretend before God, and the isolation that comes from not being at peace with him. A heart that is truly free—forgiven and declared righteous in Christ—is the "upright heart" David speaks of in the final words of Psalm 32. Such a heart can experience God's precious love and walk faithfully with him.

Bibliography

Aristotle. *Nicomachean Ethics*. Edited by Roger Crisp. Revised edition. Cambridge: Cambridge University Press, 2014.

Augustine. *The Confessions*. Translated by John K. Ryan. New York, NY: Image, 2014.

———. *Handbook on Faith, Hope, and Love*. Translated by Albert C. Outler. Christian Classics Ethereal Library. Accessed February 19, 2025. https://ccel.org/ccel/augustine/enchiridion/enchiridion.chapter3.html.

Brumley, Albert E. "This World Is Not My Home." 1919. https://mobilehymns.org/english/This_World_Is_Not_My_Home.html.

Bonhoeffer, Dietrich. *Discipleship*. Vol. 4 of *Dietrich Bonhoeffer Works*. Minneapolis, MN: Fortress Press, 2001.

———. *Meditating on the Word*. Edited and translated by David Gracie. Cambridge, MA: Cowley Publications, 1986.

———. *Psalms: The Prayer Book of the Bible*. Minneapolis, MN: Broadleaf Books, 2022.

Brueggemann, Walter. *Introduction to Psalms: The Prayer Book of the Bible*, by Dietrich Bonhoeffer. Minneapolis, MN: Broadleaf Books, 2022.

Cohen, Leonard. "Anthem." *Genius*. Accessed June 20, 2025. https://genius.com/Leonard-cohen-anthem-lyrics.

Craigie, Peter C. *Psalms 1–50*. Vol. 19. Word Biblical Commentary. Dallas: Word, Incorporated, 1983.

Ellsworth, Roger. *Opening up Psalms*. Opening Up Commentary. Leominster: Day One Publications, 2006.

Evans, Stephen. *Pocket Dictionary of Apologetics & Philosophy of Religion*. Downers Grove, IL: InterVarsity Press, 2002.

Gingrich, Roy E. *The Book of Psalms (Book One)*. Memphis, TN: Riverside Printing, 2005.

Grudem, Wayne. *Systematic Theology*. Grand Rapids, MI: Zondervan, 2000. Kindle.

"Guilt." *Psychology Today*. Accessed April 19, 2025. https://www.psychologytoday.com/us/basics/guilt.

Bibliography

Guzik, David. "Study Guide for Psalm 32." *Blue Letter Bible.* Accessed January 22, 2025. https://www.blueletterbible.org/comm/guzik_david/study-guide/psalm/psalm-32.cfm.

Hall, Dudley. *Grace Works.* Sisters, OR: Multnomah Publishers, 2000.

Henry, Matthew. *Matthew Henry's Concise Commentary.* Oak Harbor, WA: Logos Research Systems, 1997.

Kempis, Thomas à. *The Imitation of Christ.* Edited by Paul M. Bechtel. Chicago: Moody Press, 1984.

Lange, John Peter, et al. *A Commentary on the Holy Scriptures: Psalms.* Bellingham, WA: Logos Bible Software, 2008.

Lewis, C.S. *The Great Divorce.* San Francisco: HarperSanFrancisco, 2001.

———. *Letters to Malcolm: Chiefly on Prayer.* New York: Harcourt Brace Jovanovich, 1964.

———. *The Lion, the Witch and the Wardrobe.* London: Collins, 1997.

———. *The Magician's Nephew.* London: Collins, 1997.

———. *Mere Christianity.* In The C.S. Lewis Signature Classics, 1–256. New York: HarperOne, 2017.

———. *The Weight of Glory.* New York, NY: HarperCollins, 2009. Everand.

Lloyd-Jones, Sally. *The Jesus Storybook Bible.* Grand Rapids, MI: Zonderkidz, 2007.

Longman, Tremper III. *Psalms: An Introduction and Commentary.* Edited by David G. Firth. Vol. 15–16. *Tyndale Old Testament Commentaries.* Nottingham, England: Inter-Varsity Press, 2014.

MacArthur, John Jr. *The MacArthur Study Bible.* Electronic ed. Nashville, TN: Word Pub., 1997.

MacDonald, William. *Believer's Bible Commentary: Old and New Testaments.* Edited by Arthur Farstad. Nashville: Thomas Nelson Publishers, 1995. Accessed via Logos Bible Software.

McCracken, H.P. "Isaiah 43:25." *Tabletalk Magazine,* August 2019. Accessed February 21, 2025. https://tabletalkmagazine.com/article/2019/08/isaiah-4325.

Plato. *Five Dialogues.* 2nd ed. Translated by G. M. A. Grube. Revised by John M. Cooper. Indianapolis: Hackett Publishing, 2002.

Radmacher, Earl D., Ronald Barclay Allen, and H. Wayne House. *The Nelson Study Bible: New King James Version.* Nashville: T. Nelson Publishers, 1997. Logos.

Rosen, Michael. *We're Going on a Bear Hunt.* New York: Aladdin Paperbacks, 2003.

Spurgeon, Charles. "Confession of Sin." In *Spurgeon's Sermons, Volume 3.* Grand Rapids, MI: Baker Book House, 1987.

———. *The Treasury of David: Psalms 27–57.* Vol. 2. London; Edinburgh; New York: Marshall Brothers, n.d.

Ten Boom, Corrie. *The Hiding Place.* Bloomington, MN: Chosen Books, 2006.

Thompson, Francis. "The Hound of Heaven." Accessed December 5, 2024. http://www.houndofheaven.com/poem.

BIBLIOGRAPHY

Tozer, A.W. *The Knowledge of the Holy*. New York: Harper & Brothers, 1961.

Tripp, Paul. "Psalm 32: The Blessing of Confession and Forgiveness." Paul Tripp Ministries Blog. September 18, 2023. https://www.paultripp.com/psalms/posts/psalm-32-the-blessing-of-confession-and-forgiveness.

Waltke, Bruce K. "Psalms 1–41." *The Gospel Coalition Commentary*. Accessed January 27, 2025. https://www.thegospelcoalition.org/commentary/psalm-1-psalm-41/.

Waltke, Bruce K., James M. Houston, and Erika Moore. *The Psalms as Christian Lament: A Historical Commentary*. Grand Rapids, MI; Cambridge, U.K.: William B. Eerdmans Publishing Company, 2014.

Waltner, James H. *Psalms*. Believers Church Bible Commentary. Scottdale, PA; Waterloo, ON: Herald Press, 2006.

Wiersbe, Warren W. *With the Word Bible Commentary*. Nashville: Thomas Nelson, 1991.

Wilcock, Michael. *The Message of Psalms: Songs for the People of God*. Edited by J. A. Motyer. Vol. 1. The Bible Speaks Today. Nottingham, England: Inter-Varsity Press, 2001.

Wilkerson, Bruce, and Kenneth Boa. *Talk Thru the Bible*. Nashville, TN: Thomas Nelson, 2002.

www.ingramcontent.com/pod-product-compliance
Lightning Source LLC
Chambersburg PA
CBHW070313110426
42738CB00052B/2492